# GREENPRINTS

## FOR CHANGING SCHOOLS

SUE GREIG    GRAHAM PIKE    DAVID SELBY

**WWF**

**Kogan Page**

# Acknowledgements

The authors would like to thank the many advisers, teachers and students, from Bradford, Cornwall, Devon, Dorset, Leeds, Newcastle and North Tyneside LEAs and external agency workers who agreed to be interviewed. Particular thanks are due to those named individuals and institutions featured in the Case Studies. The authors are also indebted to those teachers and students who allowed the photographers into their classrooms.

Special thanks are owed to Sue Coward, secretary to the Global Impact Project, for her meticulous transcribing of tapes; and to Gail Slavin and Vicky Matthews, Centre secretaries, for their valiant work in preparing the manuscript under tremendous pressure.

This book draws on the three year project entitled 'Global Impact', carried out on behalf of WWF United Kingdom by the Centre for Global Education.

Sue Greig and Graham Pike are Research Fellows, David Selby is Director, at the Centre for Global Education, University of York, Heslington, York YO1 5DD

Co-published in 1989 by
The World Wide Fund For Nature
and
Kogan Page Ltd, 120 Pentonville Road, London N1 9JN

Copyright © The World Wide Fund For Nature, 1989
ISBN 1–85091–950–X [Kogan Page]
ISBN 0–947613–08–0 [World Wide Fund]

Typeset by Input Typesetting, London
Printed and bound in Great Britain by
Biddles Ltd, Guildford and King's Lynn

Design by: Schermuly Design Co.

# Contents

Pamela Venus

# CHAPTER ONE

# A Greening of Education

## Picture an oak tree and a girl blowing bubbles . . .

Picture an oak tree standing in a school field somewhere in the United Kingdom. Under the tree sits a girl blowing bubbles, laughing as they drift gently away on the breeze catching the sunlight.

Consider the tree. On first reflection, it appears to stand fixed, separate and independent. A whole tree and nothing but a tree. Yet, recognizable though it is in its tree-form, almost all the materials and energy needed to make it grow are in continuous exchange with the surrounding environment. Earth, air, water and sunlight are in constant interplay in sustaining its existence. Nutrients from a dead bird lying by its roots will begin their journey through the tree next summer; the leaves shed in the autumn will help nourish the earth next spring. Things flow into one another. . . .

Consider the United Kingdom. Standing in its island separateness, its politicians, its media, its school textbooks still talk of 'national sovereignty', of 'national interest', of 'national culture'. Yet, in the final analysis, we are hard pressed to give real meaning to the rhetoric. In a world of multi-layered interconnections and interdependencies between lands and peoples, our 'Britishness' includes 'foreign' food, 'foreign' goods, 'foreign' television programmes; our environmental problems are other countries' environmental problems and theirs ours; our citizens share solidarity and identity with peoples scattered around the world. The United Kingdom, in short, depends for its ever-changing identity and meaning upon its dynamic relationship with other parts of the global system. To maintain concepts such as national sovereignty against the plain fact of mutual interdependence necessarily involves distortion and self-deception (forms of self-censorship, propaganda, signs declaring 'Made in Britain' which tell only half the truth). Things flow into one another. . . .

Consider the girl blowing bubbles. In the iridescent skin of each bubble is the reflection of what lies beyond; the girl, the tree, the field, the sun's rays. What delights the girl in the bubble has no existence in its own right. The bubble owes its brief life to the will of the girl; its fleeting beauty is both a gift from a world larger than itself and a gift to that world. The girl, too, owes her meaning and identity to her connectedness with worlds beyond herself. Energy, matter, ideas and information flow in and out of her. Her physical and mental health depend on the quality of relationships she enjoys with people and place – her parents and relatives, her friends, her community, the places she works and plays in, walks through, talks and dreams about. Her life, her expectations and perceptions, her emerging image of herself as a woman, are forever being shaped by events and trends within a seamless global system.

During the last three hundred years the Western world has, by and large, disregarded the connectedness of things. Students in school learn about trees by identifying and studying the characteristics and behaviour of their separate parts. To recognize all the parts, the message goes, is to know the whole. In lesson after lesson they learn a 'national' history largely decontextualised from the interplay of events in the wider world. In science lessons they learn that a bubble is a phenomenon arising out of the viscous properties of molecules. They pick up, too, through both the overt and covert agenda of their formal and informal education that human experience can be carved up into separate parts (historical, geographic, scientific, technical and so on) and studied separately; that mind can be separated from body; that reason is divorced from emotion; that human beings are set apart from and stand above the natural world. The girl under the tree goes to a doctor when she has a particular physical complaint, for instance, a painful foot. The doctor treats the foot – the part – often paying scant attention to the girl's general physical condition and even less to her emotional and mental state and to any environmental factors, broadly defined, which might impinge upon her condition. At school, the girl's intellectual development is administered to in 'academic' lessons, her bodily health in physical education and games lessons and her emotional and social problems by an 'academic' teacher briefly donning her 'pastoral' hat for the duration of tutor time. It is as though we have placed ourselves within a conceptual bubble, the walls of which obscure rather than help us see the connectedness within ourselves and between ourselves and the rest of the planet.

A growing number of contemporary thinkers attribute the many global ecological and social crises we are now facing to the pervasiveness of fragmentationalist thinking. Acid rain, the 'greenhouse effect', the deterioration of the ozone layer, the destruction of the rainforests, the widening gulf between rich and poor, the poisoning of the seas, the spread of deserts, the proliferation of weaponry, the wholesale destruction of species, race and gender inequality, they argue, have their root cause in a worldview originating in the West but now girdling the globe on account of Western power and influence. 'The dominant worldview – materialist, rationalist, utilitarian and reductionist – has held sway for two or three centuries,' write Dorothy and Walter Schwarz. 'It has given many of us wealth and freedom but the dramatic cost is evident in the irreversible damage wreaked by "development" on our planet.'[1] 'Inner fragmentation,' writes Fritjof Capra, 'mirrors our view of the world "outside" which is seen as a multitude of separate objects and events. The natural environment is treated as if it consisted of separate parts to be exploited by different interest groups. The fragmented view is further extended to society which is split into different nations, races, religious and political groups. The belief that all these fragments – in ourselves, in our environment and in our society – are really separate can be seen as the essential reason for the present series of social, ecological and cultural crises. It has alienated us from nature and from our fellow human beings. It has brought a grossly unjust distribution of natural resources creating economic and political disorder; an ever rising wave of violence, both spontaneous and institutionalised, and an ugly, polluted environment in which life has often become physically and mentally unhealthy.'[2]

The fragmentationalist worldview arose out of the ideas of a number of eminent philosophers and scientists during the Western scientific revolution of the seventeenth and early eighteenth century. Over the succeeding two centuries it progressively colonised and informed other areas of Western thought and expertise such as economics, medicine and social science. Its arch-proponent was René Descartes. His thinking, captured in his famous statement, '*Cogito, ergo sum*' ('I think, therefore I exist'), carried profound implications for how we see ourselves and our relationship with

*The major problems in the world are the result of the difference between the way nature works and the way man thinks.*

– Gregory Bateson

the environment. It divided self from world. It led Westerners to equate personal meaning and identity primarily with their mind rather than with their body, mind and environment in relationship. It established an inner hierarchy in which mind (the rational, the cerebral) was separate from and superior to the bodily, the spiritual, the emotional and the intuitive. It disconnected the human observer from things to be observed in nature and, through that divorce, accorded the scientific mind with the quality of pure objectivity. It denied that the environment had an important part to play in investing our lives, individually and collectively, with meaning. The environment, relegated to an inferior place in the Cartesian division of mind and matter, became a vast pool of organic and inorganic materials appropriate for exploitation. As Gregory Bateson puts it: 'As you arrogate all mind to yourself, you will see the world around you as mindless and therefore not entitled to moral and ethical consideration. The environment will seem yours to exploit.'[3]

---

*It is in intentionality and will that the human being experiences his identity. 'I' is the 'I' of 'I can.' Descartes was wrong when he wrote, 'I think, therefore I am,' for identity does not come out of thinking as such, and certainly not out of intellectualization. Descartes' formulation leaves out exactly the variable that is most significant; it jumps from thought to identity, when what actually occurs is the intermediate variable of 'I can.' What happens in human experiences is 'I conceive-I can-I will-I am.' The 'I can' and 'I will' are the essential experiences of identity.*

– Rollo May

---

*But ask now the beasts and they shall teach thee; and the fowls of the air, and they shall teach thee; Or speak to the earth and it shall teach thee; and the fishes of the sea shall declare unto thee;*
– Book of Job

An alternative source of inspiration for Christians. A useful book on Christianity and the environment is Sean McDonagh, *To Care for the Earth – A Call to a New Theology*, Geoffrey Chapman, 1986.

The seeds that Descartes scattered found congenial ground in a Western Christian world in which there had been a long and generally dominant tradition of human-centredness. 'And God said, Let us make man in our image, after our likeness: and let them have dominion over the fish of the sea, and over the fowl of the air, and over the cattle, and over all the Earth, and over every creeping thing that creepeth upon the Earth' (*Book of Genesis*). This passage had helped legitimize a dualism between 'man' and nature; it fuelled the view, too, that 'man' held a monopoly of spirit and that 'man' was justified in his exploitation of the Earth. An alternative strand within Christian thinking – which spoke of stewardship of nature – has frequently cried to be heard but to little avail.

For Descartes, and for Isaac Newton after him, that which is not mind is machine. The human body, animals, plants, the natural world are mechanical; like a machine they are perfectly understandable by reducing them to their separate component parts. The human mind, working within but separate from its machine-body, can come to an understanding of the multiplicity of machines making up the environment through scientific enquiry and analysis; to meet any desired end, human beings can handle the environment in very much the same utilitarian way as mechanics approach their machines. Arising inevitably out of the fragmentationalist – or mechanistic – worldview is also an acceptance of linear causality (machine part X strikes machine part Y and Y strikes Z), a linear unidirectional conception of time and a confident belief – shared by capitalist and communist states alike – that to extend our control over the earth will lead to a 'better' (for which read 'more material') future.

'It is usually said,' writes Huston Smith, 'that the Copernican revolution humbled man by displacing him from the center of the universe, but this spatial dislodgement was nothing compared with the arrogance that followed in its wake, the arrogance of assuming that nothing exists that quite equals ourselves.'[4] Our ecological and social crises now call for another revolution of Copernican proportions, for the displacement of a dominant worldview that sets human beings apart from and above the myriad lifeforms making up this planet. A shift is needed from such an anthropocentric (person-centred) philosophy with its built-in 'biospheric inegalitarianism', to a biocentric (life-centred) philosophy which humbly recognises that we are within the environment; that reverence rather than ruthlessness is due to the natural world; that, however special and significant, we are but one creature in an incredibly complex and seamless web of life.

In recent times this holistic way of seeing the world has been embraced by increasing numbers within Western societies with a consequent rejection of the values of the dominant fragmentationalist worldview (values such as competition, control, domination, exploitation and rampant materialism). The concept of *holism* – the word interestingly shares the same root as words such as 'holy', 'hale' and 'healthy' – has been particularly nourished by developments in sub-atomic physics, ecological and feminist thinking and mounting interest in Eastern religions and philosophies and the worldviews of indigenous peoples. Physicists have discovered that there is no final separate and indissoluble 'building block' of matter, that sub-atomic

*What the world needs now is a sense of humus.*
– David Dufty

reality is indivisible, that the behaviour and characteristics of particles have no meaning save in dynamic interaction with their surrounding sub-atomic environment. As a result, many have taken on board an ever more holistic interpretation of reality and have begun to ask themselves whether matter is, in fact, ultimately matter or a form of consciousness pervading everything. The categorical mind/matter dichotomy of Descartes has begun to look very poorly indeed! Likewise, work in sub-atomic physics has obliterated the Cartesian notion that the observer is removed from what she observes. The properties that a sub-atomic particle displays, it has become clear, depend on the particular questions asked of it (as expressed in the construction of the experiment) and, hence, the values and priorities of the observer. 'We have left behind a universe where the observer *observes* the observed,' write John Briggs and David Peat, 'and have entered a looking glass, a universe where, in some way (we can only see this part very dimly now) the *observer is observed.*'[5] For the most satisfying expression of their findings, sub-atomic physicists have increasingly turned to the writings of Eastern mystics where all things and events are perceived of as but different manifestations of one ultimate reality.[6]

David Bohm, a physicist at the very frontier of his field, proposes that a hidden order is at work behind the visible and seemingly separate forms that we all recognise in the world around us (the *explicate* order). This *implicate* order is the flowing unbroken whole – or holomovement – from which things that are manifest have unfolded and into which they finally refold. Bohm suggests that the future is carried as yet unfolded within the implicate order and can thus be regarded as effectively co-present. At a profounder and yet more subtle *super-implicate* level, matter and consciousness become fused into one. The implicate levels are thus an all-encompassing background to our physical, psychological and spiritual experience.[7] In Bohm's judgement, human beings need to be more alive and responsive to implicate realities in their understanding of their own identity, their social relationships and their relationship with the environment. A blindness to our essential connectedness with everything and everyone else is ultimately self-destructive. Bohm reminds us that the word 'individual' means undivided; hence 'individuality is only possible if it unfolds from wholeness'.[8] A person who fails to connect with the whole (more correctly described as a 'dividual') must necessarily do harm to her own nature just as whole societies ultimately do themselves harm if they ignore the needs of other societies or if they plough a lone anthropocentric furrow that erodes the health of the

planet.[9] Bohm asks that, like the bubbles blown by the girl
under the oak tree, we display a 'transparence with respect
to the whole'.[10] Elsewhere, he urges upon us 'passionate
insight' by which he means an insight 'that penetrates
beyond the fixities and particulars of the given to an underlying wholeness that is the source of all genuine knowledge'
and that, simultaneously, drives us to look inwards upon
ourselves as learners engaged in the process of learning.[11]

> *In order to be at home in the world, we must be fully of
> it, experiencing it directly as mud between our toes, as the
> rough bark on a tree, as the song of the world awakening
> every morning. The Earth speaks to something in each
> and every person, even when we are imprisoned by
> concrete and steel. In that dialogue lies a form of
> celebration as primitively powerful as anything to be
> found in our anaemic, emaciated culture.*
>
> – Jonathon Porritt & David Winner,
> *The Coming of the Greens*

At this point Bohm brushes against a theme of crucial
importance to those sharing an holistic worldview – that the
achievement of full and authentic personhood is intimately
bound up with the health of the planet. The defence of the
environment, Neil Evernden points out, is ultimately a
defence of meaning.[12] Divorce ourselves from the environment and we lose something essential to our identity. Waste
away the environment and we waste away ourselves. Our
inner fragmentation of mind and body and our relegation
of the emotional, intuitive and spiritual in favour of the
intellectual is to distort and repress our potential from
which arises discord between ourselves and nature. A full
and undistorted realisation of personal potential (in which
the rational and cerebral would be in complementary and
synergistic relationship with the emotional, intuitive and
spiritual) would, on the other hand, enable us to match
our needs with those of the planet.[13] Whole persons, whole
planet. Viewed another way, we can say that an holistic

> *Ecological thinking . . . requires a kind of vision across
> boundaries. The epidermis of the skin is ecologically like
> a pond surface or a forest soil, not a shell so much as
> delicate interpenetration. It reveals the self enabled and
> extended . . . as part of the landscape and the ecosystem,
> because the beauty and complexity of nature are
> continuous with ourselves . . . we must affirm that the
> world is a being, a part of our own body.*
>
> – Paul Shepard, *The Subversive Science*

worldview calls for a reconceptualisation of what it means to be a healthy human being. Real health is not a question of going to the doctor when a particular disease assails us or when a particular bodily part breaks down, but of increasing – and acting upon – our awareness of the 'interconnectedness' of body, mind and spirit and of the 'interconnectedness' between ourselves, the rest of human-kind and our environment (including people and places thousands of miles away).

> *We used to think that Marxism or feminism held the answers to all our problems. We thought, 'If only we can get rid of racism, change capitalism and educate people, everything will be different.' But now we know those hopes and aspirations left out something fundamental. They failed because they failed to take account of the earth we walk on. Without the earth, we have nothing. Our Utopian concepts are flying out of the sky. So we have to rethink all our ideas in a new framework.*
>
> – Fay Weldon

The sense of alienation afflicting contemporary society is viewed by holistic thinkers as having its source within the worldview inherited from Descartes. The social convulsions we are experiencing and the ineffectual convolutions of 'experts' and 'authorities' as they seek solutions, will not go away unless we divest ourselves of fragmentationalist orthodoxies. 'While the West's "brain" rolls ever further down the reductionist path,' writes Huston Smith, 'other centres of society – our emotions, for example, as they find expression through artists, and our wills, as evidenced in part by rise in crime and senseless vandalism – protest. These other centres of our selves feel that they are being dragged, kicking and screaming, down an ever-darkening tunnel. We need to listen to their protests, for they force us to ask if it is possible to move toward a world view that, without compromising reason or evidence in the slightest, would allow more room to the sides of our selves that our current world view constricts.'[15] Ivan Illich has mounted a sustained and telling attack on social progress as engineered by experts. He calls for a 'convivial' society marked by an emphasis on human relationships, personal intimacy and a shedding of technocratic assumptions.[16] A profound cultural transformation, no less, is needed.

Woven within that transformation must be a 'revaluation of the feminine'.[17] The fragmentationalist worldview has served to reinforce, validate and inflate qualities and behaviours that we have been conditioned to regard as masculine

> *When a person forgets that all creation is a unity, allegiance goes to lesser wholes such as the family, the home team, or the company.*
>
> *Nationalism, racism, classism, sexism; all arise as consciousness of unity is lost. People take sides and favour this versus that.*
>
> – John Heider,
> *The Tao of Leadership*

*Many feminists are discovering that it is not enough to secure positions of power within the current masculinist structure because this is in effect only changing the content and not the form. They have begun to apply their perspectives and visions as feminists towards creating an entirely new blueprint for society. . . . As the domination of mankind continues to erode the balance and beauty of the earth, it is of the utmost urgency that we cease arguing over semantics and differences of opinions. We must turn our energies towards creating a consciousness of wholeness, in which we are concerned with relationship rather than difference, and in which we may learn how best to live together and to cultivate the earth out of love and a conscious understanding of the harmony of life.*

– Stephanie Leland

(such as analysis, reason, assertiveness, aggression, competitiveness, exploitation, a proclivity for hierarchies, hunger for domination). Other qualities and behaviours, traditionally regarded as feminine (such as synthesis, seeing things in wholes, empathy, emotion, intuition, co-operation, active democracy, receptivity, nurturing) have been downgraded or marginalised. Our current ecological crises can be perceived of as adding up to 'a crisis of masculine values'.[18] A more ecological approach to ourselves, each other and the environment would necessitate the dethronement of such values. Liberation from patriarchy and the achievement of a 'right' relationship with nature are, thus, complementary goals. James Robertson has written of his preference for a Sane, Humane, Ecological (SHE) future, the acronym conveying the need for a future marked by feminine modes of perceiving, doing and being.[19] The 'revaluation of the feminine', we have often been reminded, is not about women adopting the role of ersatz men with their 'disastrous masculine technocracy' left untouched but rather a question of rejecting fragmentationalism and achieving a creative tension and interplay in all of us of masculine and feminine qualities, of the assertive and the integrative.[20] Given the substitution by Descartes, Newton and others of 'a mechanistic for the ancient organic and female concept of nature', it is not surprising, suggests Margarita Bowen, that we should now see a conjunction of interest between the conservation, ecology and feminist movements.[21]

A worldview that takes as its starting point the idea that everything in the skies, on the earth and under the earth is 'penetrated with connectedness and relatedness'[22] has about it something that is profoundly spiritual. Jonathon Porritt,

*The new hero will be Centauric, (i.e. linking the mental to the spiritual) wholebodied, mentally androgenous, psychic, intuitive and rational, male and female, and the lead in this new development I believe can come most easily from the female, since our society is already grossly male over-adapted. . . .*

– Cherie McCusker

*Know this Atman*
*Unborn, undying,*
*Never ceasing,*
*Never beginning,*
*Deathless, birthless,*
*Unchanging for ever.*
*How can It die*
*The death of the body?*

*Knowing It birthless,*
*Knowing It deathless,*
*Knowing it endless,*
*For ever unchanging,*
*Dream not you do*
*The deed of the killer,*
*Dream not the power*
*Is yours to command it.*

*Worn-out garments*
*Are shed by the body:*
*Worn-out bodies*
*Are shed by the dweller*
*Within the body*
*New bodies are donned*
*By the dweller, like*
*garments.*

*Not wounded by weapons,*
*Not burned by fire,*
*Not dried by the wind,*
*Not wetted by water:*
*Such is the Atman,*

*Not dried not wetted,*
*Not burned, not wounded,*
*Innermost element,*
*Everywhere, always,*
*Being of beings,*
*Changeless, eternal,*
*For ever and ever.*

– Krishna, *Bhagavad Gita*

borrowing from Fritz Schumacher, has called the process towards holism one of 'metaphysical reconstruction' in which we become whole human beings by recognising 'the holistic interrelatedness of life on Earth'.[23] Porritt's call finds a deep resonance in Hindu thought. *Brahman*, the ultimate reality behind everything in the world, finds expression in the human soul as *Atman*. *Brahman* and *Atman* are one. The creative play of the divine, called *lila*, gives us the world we see. To 'confuse the myriad forms of the divine *lila* with reality, without perceiving the unity of *Brahman* underlying all these forms' is to be 'under the spell of *maya*' (i.e. to be living with an illusion of reality). To break free from *maya*'s spell and 'to experience, concretely and personally, that everything, including our own self, is *Brahman*' is *moksha* or 'liberation'.[24] The holistic worldview calls for us to go through such a process of liberation and enlightenment.

A number of holistic thinkers have written of the consciousness they regard as pervading everything, organic and inorganic. For Gregory Bateson, there is a universal mind 'immanent in the total interconnected social system · and planetary ecology' of which the human mind is but a sub-system.[25] For James Lovelock, the earth is a single intelligent organism which defines and regulates conditions necessary for its survival. Humans need to recognise that they are but one partner within Gaia (the ancient Greek goddess of the earth) and a dangerous partner at that. 'From a Gaian viewpoint,' writes Lovelock, 'all attempts to rationalize a subjugated biosphere with man in charge are as doomed to failure as the similar concept of benevolent colonialism. They all assume that man is the possessor of this planet; if not the owner, then the tenant. . . . The Gaia hypothesis implies that the stable state of our planet includes man as a part of, or partner in, a very democratic entity.'[26] Peter Russell unites the Gaia principle with the notion that human beings stand on the threshold of an evolutionary leap. A reconciliation with Gaia arising out of humanity's evolution into 'a healthy, integrated social super-organism' would signal the development of the 'high synergy society' in which greater diversity amongst individuals would co-exist alongside a larger sense of oneness with others and the environment ('we would begin to feel for the rest of the world in much the same way that we feel for our own bodies – we would find it as crazy to decimate the equatorial rainforests for some short-term end, as it would be to cut off a finger').[27] Whether or not we go along with the speculations and theories of leading edge thinkers such as Bateson, Lovelock and Russell, it is crucial for planetary survival that we recognise that 'the Earth speaks to something in all of us, and each of us needs some special place where we can hear the song of Gaia, where the "living continuity of person and planet" becomes an effortless part of us.'[28]

An holistic worldview asks that we tread lightly on the earth; that we rediscover the wisdoms lost to most of us but still preserved amongst those indigenous peoples who have managed to resist world-girdling fragmentationalism; that we embrace a deep ecological viewpoint and recognize that everything on this planet has a value extrinsic to human needs. It calls on us to embrace 'ecology in all its biocentric, holistic fullness, seeing humankind as just one strand in the seamless web of creation, not above or outside creation but miraculously incorporate within it.'[29] A shift of worldview, it bears repetition, will enable us to rediscover lost potentials within ourselves. For children not yet immersed in a fragmentationalist mindset, the process could be as much one of discovery as rediscovery. The question then arises: what can school do for that girl under the oak tree blowing bubbles?

> *'I am protecting the rainforest' develops to 'I am that part of the rainforest protecting myself. I am that part of the rainforest recently emerged into thinking.' What a relief then! The thousands of years of imagined separation are over and we begin to recall our true nature.*
> – John Seed,
> *Thinking Like a Mountain*

---

> *A good friend of mine who was a social worker had to go up the mountains of Luzon . . . to conduct a census of the Negritoes, our own Aborigines. My friend was accompanied by a young Negrito guide and as they treaded through the slopes they passed by guava trees, papayas and wild berry trees, all heavy with fruits. . . . The Negrito guide picked one fruit and offered it to my friend as he took one for himself. Unable to resist the temptation of ripe guavas hanging freely from spreading branches, my friend took out her bag and filled it to bursting capacity . . . the guide looked in disbelief and almost in outrage, saying:*
>
> *'How can you pick more than you can eat at the time? What will others eat when they get hungry? These fruits do not belong to you alone. This mountain and everything in it, belongs to everyone – our sisters, our brothers, the deer and the birds, to everyone who needs food and a piece of the earth to sleep on.*
> – Virginia Cawagas, Executive Secretary of the Catholic Educational Association of the Philippines

## Two Worldviews: A Checklist of Some Key Features

| The Fragmentationalist Worldview | The Holistic Worldview |
| --- | --- |
| An emphasis on separateness and disconnectedness. Wholes are made up of separate parts; the whole is no more, no less, than the sum of its parts. That parts interact does not qualitatively influence the whole. We are separate from other peoples and the global environment. | An emphasis on connectedness. Parts are only finally understandable if viewed in dynamic relationship with all other parts. The combined interaction of all the parts creates an organic whole which is greater than the sum of their individual effects. We are profoundly connected to other peoples and the global environment. |
| A preference for analysis and reduction (understanding things by reducing them to their separate parts). | A preference for synthesis, integration, the synoptic. |
| The observer is separate from what she observes; complete objectivity is achievable. | Observer and observed are intimately connected. What is observed, how it is observed and resulting interpretations are influenced by the observer's priorities, values and framework of thought. The observer is to some degree observing herself; she is neither 'outside', 'neutral' or 'objective'. |
| The rational and cerebral are separate from and superior to the emotional, the intuitive, the spiritual. | Our full potential is only realised through the dynamic and equal interplay of the rational and cerebral with the emotional, the intuitive and the spiritual. |
| Mind is separate from matter; the human mind is housed within but separate from the human body; mind and consciousness set humans apart from the rest of the planet. | Consciousness pervades everything. |

| The Fragmentationalist Worldview | The Holistic Worldview |
| --- | --- |
| Egocentrism/dividuality; identity has its source in self. | Individuality; identity arises out of a dialectic between self and whole. We achieve the highest level of individuality when we reflect the whole. |
| Outer-directedness; we look out on the world and seek to understand it. The focus is on change external to the person. | Outer- and inner-directedness; a 'journey outwards' to understand the world requires a reciprocal 'journey inwards' to understand self and self in the world. The focus is on personal growth and transformation as much as social/environmental change. |
| Patriarchal values; masculine behaviours and qualities prized; feminine behaviours and qualities devalued. | Post-patriarchal values; a tensile, yet creative, integration of masculine and feminine behaviours and qualities. |
| Emphasis on hierarchical, centralised, inegalitarian structures, competitive relationships and representative democracy; reliance/dependency upon authority and experts. A 'control' mindset. | Emphasis on non-hierarchical, decentralised, egalitarian structures and collegial/co-operative relationships, participative involvement and direct, consensual democracy. A liberationist, empowering mindset. |
| Anthropocentric; humankind seen as the principal actor on the planet; plant and animal species and inorganic matter accorded value only in terms of human priorities and needs. | Biocentric; humankind seen as but one element within the planet's system; plant and animal species and inorganic matter have their own intrinsic value. |
| Separateness from, domination and control over, nature; an exploitative ruthlessness towards the environment. | Oneness with nature; reverence towards the environment. |

# Back to Basics

Pamela Venus

Forsaking the oak tree, the girl returns to an engine room of the fragmentationalist worldview. Her learning is compartmentalised into constricted frameworks of study, each with its own label, self-referential programme and tidy rationale. There is little time for encouragement to explore the connections she occasionally perceives between what she learns in one lesson and the next. She has learnt that teachers ('experts') talk a lot, that they give out a body of 'right' information and that lessons revolve around them. She has picked up, too, that what matters most in school is what is readily quantifiable and testable. Doing well in school is about competing, about recalling facts and ideas, about finding meaning through analysis ('comprehension' work is about matching the right bits in the passage with the right question), about understanding how a succession of stages or events led on to or caused one another. She has learnt that in most subjects the communication of personal feelings is best avoided. For efficiency's sake, teachers are happy to permit a modicum of ritualized interpersonal banter but a meaningful exchange of inner feelings is, in most circumstances, considered inappropriate. Intuition, daydreaming, fantasy, guesswork and divergent thinking are, likewise, discouraged. The girl finds it odd that the big problems she learns about on television – wholesale poverty and malnutrition, environmental destruction, the denial of human rights in many countries of the world – are not picked up in school save in the odd religious or social education lesson. Her school experience leaves her with the impression that what matters most is closest to home – history and geography are mainly about England and Europe, the modern language learnt is that of our closest Western European neighbour and the books studied in English lessons are all by British writers although she is aware that English is spoken and written in many parts of the world. But, then again, the local community hardly seems to count either, in that it is a rare event for learning to take place outside school or for the classroom doors to be opened to members of the community. She would like to vent some of her feelings on these points. But where? As far as she understands it, the school is controlled by a (male) headteacher, his three (two male, one female) deputies and a number of (mainly male) heads of department. There is no platform for students to learn the skills of democratic participation even though, as they are sometimes reminded, they live in one of the best, if not the best, democracies in the world.

*Somebody said something during the election, that whatever emphasis you put on issues – green issues or anything like this – they pale into insignificance when you consider paying the next gas bill. Now you've got to get through that, because as long as people are more concerned about paying the next gas bill than the future of the planet, then we've got problems. We've got to start again in the educational process.*

– Secondary Deputy Headteacher,
Leeds

'So pervasive is the power of the institutions we have created,' writes Ivan Illich, 'that they shape not only our preferences but actually our sense of possibilities.'[30] We can see this in the education system's failure to open up discussion and reflection upon different worldviews. Students are consciously and subconsciously 'schooled' in a worldview supplied in advance. It is important that we divest ourselves of our conditioning, of the educational presuppositions, necessities and imperatives spawned by a fragmentationalist mindset, and ask ourselves what a whole-person, planet-conscious holistic education would look like.

One of the most striking features of holistic learning would be the emphasis given to *connectedness*. Bohm, we should remind ourselves, calls for a 'passionate insight' that actively seeks out the wholeness underlying any knowledge acquired. Knowledge, we all too readily assume, leads to enlightenment. The mass of information in the modern world encourages specialisation; it entices each and every one of us to gather and marshall our own particular constellation of useful facts. 'Our professionals have become like thousands of little creatures poking their sticks furiously at different parts of the elephant, and with a different notion of what the beast must look like. The more they poke at the little space reserved for them, the more convinced they are that they know what they are poking at, and the more wrong they become.'[31] The pursuit of knowledge can thus lead to what Bohm calls 'endarkenment', a failure to relate the particular to the whole.[32] An holistic education replaces the notion of collecting, storing, exploiting and imparting 'stocks of isolated facts' with 'the idea of examining the *flow* of interconnected phenomena. . . . The external world will be examined not as a series of isolated causal relationships, but as a web of interrelated phenomena expressing many possible scenarios for movement and change.'[33] Put another way, we can talk of the fragmentationalist curricu-

*What I'm really concerned to do is to change children's attitudes towards their natural environment because this is the Earth they live on, it's the only Earth they've got and they're the people when they grow up who can do something about the way the world is being poisoned and slowly destroyed, and if we can start them off at nine and ten planting trees and looking after tadpoles and growing wild flowers and things like that, respecting the birds and so on, not shooting them, then we're starting now, we're beginning to win.*

– Deputy Headteacher, Leeds Middle School

lum obstructing and the holistic curriculum enhancing
*comprehension* (literally, 'the ability to hold it all
together').[34] Holistic education does not necessarily depend
upon a rearrangement of the curriculum, a shift to interdisciplinary timetable slots, although that might well help;
it calls, rather, for an attitude of mind on the part of
teacher and student alike which prioritises and searches out
relatedness to the whole.

The holistic curriculum would help students acquire what
Charlene Spretnak calls 'biocentric wisdom'[35]: an understanding that we are part of, not above, nature; that there
is an essential unity between all life-forms, that all species
have intrinsic value; that we have a responsibility to live
within the ecological and resource limits of the planet. It
would encompass a global perspective through continued
demonstration of the interdependence of lands and peoples
and of the interlocking nature of key global issues. As such,
it would involve a dynamic refocussing of some of the most
important developments in social and political education
over the last thirty years (particularly development education, environmental education, human rights education
and peace education). It would also have a strong futures
orientation. Students would explore possible, probable and
preferred futures – personal to global – and learn and practice the skills necessary to help bring about their preferred
future scenarios.[36] Underpinning the curriculum would be
a concern to develop personal, social and environmental
responsibility; a respect for diversity within an acceptance
of commonality; a concern for justice, equality and peace;
an expression of solidarity with peoples across the globe;
and a recognition that 'acting morally is acting in a way
that future generations would ask us to act if they were
here to ask.'[37]

Within the classroom the whole person would be
addressed. The emphasis on analytical, linear, left-brain
learning in most classrooms, with its consequent prizing
of a narrowly defined academic excellence, has had the
effect of stunting potential and devaluing diversity. Institutional support for a diversity of excellences, Douglas

*Helen Tann*

*Deciding on the sequence of photographs.*

*Helen Tann*

*In Sympathy with the Rainforest.*

Sloan suggests, 'may link education most directly with a concern for a just global society, for it demands a world in which diversity in wholeness is cherished. A holistic education demands a just and caring society.'[38] The holistic classroom would, therefore, promote whole-brain or synergistic learning giving equal status and recognition to right-brain qualities such as the ability to synthesise information, to see wholes rather than parts, to detect meaning in patterns and symbols, to personalise information, to empathise, to express emotion and draw upon intuition. The diet of teaching and learning styles regularly employed in the classroom would greatly increase; teacher input and individualised learning approaches would be offered alongside co-operative group work, experiential activities, role plays and simulations, action learning outside the classroom, imaging, guided fantasies and visualisations. 'In whole education we would decriminalize daydreaming, fantasy, inactivity and curiosity, and encourage a good deal of freedom and spontaneity.'[39] The body/mind relationship would be catered for through movement and exercise, relaxation, meditation, breathing and centering exercises (i.e. exercises aimed at harmonising body, intellect and intuition[40]). The overall ethos of the classroom would be co-operative rather than 'dividual' or competitive for it is through co-operation in the learning process that we put 'connectedness' into effect and that we come to recognise, value and learn from the diversity and interplay of perspectives and learning styles found amongst any group of learners. An overarching goal would be to foster self-esteem and group solidarity so that learning can take place within a humane, open and mutually supportive climate.

*Unfolding is endless. A millenium doesn't finish, nor does a culture, nor a project, nor a life, nor a love, nor a conference, nor a lecture. Everything, everything, everywhere, is always. . . .*
– Robin Richardson

The holistic learner would cease to genuflect before the altar of objectivity. Knowledge would be viewed as process not product or endpoint, as a matter of being, not having. The learner would recognise that knowledge comes as much from personal participation and experience as from disinterested empirical observation; that it draws upon our whole being, our values, our conscience, our senses, our intuition, our imagination. Knowledge, in short, carries 'an ethical burden'.[41] The learner would reject a mentality that uses scientific uncertainty to justify inaction (the continued preparedness on the part of government and industry to permit the release of contaminants into the atmosphere long after most of us 'know' it to be wrong is a manifestation of that mentality). As Douglas Sloan puts it: 'schools have been responsible for conveying a terrible misconception about pure objectivity, a misconception that may well account for many of the moral and ecological crises which now press so relentlessly upon us.'[42] In ceasing to pursue the unattainable goal of detached objectivity, the learner would see learning as a continuous journey with no fixed or final destination. 'I was partially right before and now I'm a bit more partially right.'[43] She would be conscious that decisions and judgements we reach are, by their nature, impermanent – stills taken from a moving picture that has no finale. Her understanding of the nature of knowledge would caution her against the arrogance of certainty and exhort her to be humble, iconoclastic and ever receptive to the new.

That same humility would infuse the approach of the teacher, for if learning is a process it must, by definition, be a lifelong process. The teacher's role would be that of a co-learning facilitator – a catalyst. She would be released from being a 'tour-guide' through 'the accumulated piles of so-called knowledge'[44]. She would recognise that she had much to learn from the experiences, perspectives, insights and unique cluster of potentials each of her charges brought to class; that her relationship with students should be one of symmetrical and not asymmetrical dependence.[45] The classroom climate would be open, participatory and democratic with students involved in the negotiation and evaluation of the learning process. She would recognise that certain personal qualities were appropriate to her decentered role as facilitator: a healthy level of self-esteem; a positive view of human nature; the ability to trust in the capacity of others to think and learn for themselves; a preparedness to let go; a lack of defensiveness; a readiness to acknowledge her mistakes and to be seen learning from them. Crucially, she would need to divest herself of the control mentality responsible for so much stress and alienation in our schools.

Holistic education is about developing whole people for a whole planet. It offers vision, seeks to liberate and empower the individual and promotes active global citizenship and environmental responsibility. In the true sense of the term, its advocates are calling upon us to go 'back to basics'; to reclaim lost forms of knowing. They are urging us to break free from a fragmentationalist mindset that has blinkered us for three hundred years and thereby rediscover ourselves, our full potential and our proper relationship with the planet. The 3Rs – the 'basics' that trip off the lips of politicians – are important, but, as David and Helen Dufty point out, basic education must also include 'one's ability to cope with one's own feelings, emotions and ego; to learn to handle jealousy and aggression and to positively reach out in love to others; to understand one's own body/mind and to be able to take responsibility for its health; to

*The task then becomes one of finding and struggling for ways that will maintain the acheivements of the modern world while at the same time recovering the sources of meaning in the primordial traditions that prevent these achievements from becoming aberrant and destructive.*

– Douglas Sloan

*I am part of the world*
*I am able to change my life*
*for the better*
*Therefore I am able to*
*change the world for the*
*better.*
– Helen & David Dufty

realise that one creates one's own reality and that one can learn to relate well to others and to have some power in life's situations; to know that one is a worthy human being of value to oneself and not just a pawn in the economic, political or personal games of those said to be "in power".'[46]

## Holistic Change

Power lies in the hands of the fragmentationalists. In all walks of life, and not least education, there are plenty of people who have a material and emotional investment in fragmentation; not wholeness. Their power derives from their position within the institution they serve but also from the fact that the structures, working and philosophy of that institution predominantly reflect the still prevailing fragmentationalist worldview. How, then, will change come about? Leading holistic thinkers say it is already happening. Fritjof Capra believes that as global crisis after global crisis demonstrates the unreality of our current way of seeing and relating to the world, a paradigm shift – a profound change in the thoughts, perceptions and values that shape our vision of reality – begins to take place. The organs of society that have successfully and creatively responded to challenge in the past begin to lose their vigour, at first partially and then more comprehensively, in the face of continually renewed challenge. The new paradigm, at first restricted to creative counter-cultural minorities, spreads and, reaching critical mass, a thorough-going cultural transformation occurs. Capra pinpoints the ecological, anti-nuclear, feminist, alternative health, human scale and human potential movements as examples of counter-cultural groups embracing the new worldview.[47] Marilyn Ferguson detects the growth of a conspiracy (literally 'a breathing together') in which unrelated groups of people are responding to our several ecological and social crises by living their lives in new ways according to a new 'Aquarian' paradigm. As more and more people embrace the new ideas and as groups connect, a collective paradigm shift occurs. The conspiracy is 'a different kind of revolution with different revolutionaries. It looks to the turnabout in consciousness of a critical number of individuals, enough to bring about a renewal of society.'[48] Jonathon Porritt and David Winner put forward a 'delta hypothesis'. Change is happening rather like change takes place in the delta of some giant river. As water flows out to sea islands of sediment build up and break the surface. Looking at the delta the islands appear separate but they are the interconnected parts of an emerging new land mass. In the same way, 'islands' of

*The sources of new dreams*
*are the 'mutants' who break*
*away from the status quo.*
– Robert Bundy

seemingly disparate groups are now questioning and discarding the values and assumptions of industrial society. These 'islands' will join up to form the emerging culture.[49]

The role of those who have already embraced the new worldview is to help the old to its gentle denouement; to do what they can to dislodge remaining obstacles to change. 'During this phase of revaluation and cultural rebirth,' writes Capra, 'it will be important to minimize the hardship, discord, and disruption that are inevitably involved in periods of great social change, and to make that transition as painless as possible. It will therefore be crucial to go beyond attacking particular social groups or institutions, and to show how their attitudes and behaviour reflect a value system that underlies our whole culture and that has now become outdated. It will be necessary to recognise and widely communicate the fact that our current social changes are manifestations of a much broader, and inevitable, cultural transformation.'[50] Marilyn Ferguson agrees. 'Long after an old paradigm has lost its value, it commands a kind of hypocritical allegiance. But if we have the courage to communicate our doubts and defection, to expose the incompleteness, the rickety structure, and the failures of the old paradigm, we can dismantle it. We don't have to wait for it to collapse on us.'[51] The process will not simply be one of total abandonment of fragmentationalism; it will be rather one of preserving that which has proved beneficial in the old paradigm (for instance, the technological wisdom we have accrued) whilst restraining or discarding those of its features which have harmed person and planet.

Those espousing the holistic worldview point to the special place of networking in effecting social and political change. Contemporary counter-cultural movements, such as the ecological and feminist movements, are characterised by similar organisational patterns. Each movement is composed of a whole international network of small, often autonomous, often grassroots, organisations, voluntarily linked together and sharing a range of basic assumptions. These 'segmented polycephalous' networks, as Virginia Hine describes them, accord with the non-hierarchical, decentralist thrust of the holistic worldview. Networking, Hine argues, 'encourages full utilisation of individual and small group innovation whilst minimising the results of failure, it promotes maximum penetration of ideas across socio-economic and cultural barriers while preserving cultural and sub-cultural diversity, it is flexible enough to adapt quickly to changing conditions, and it puts a structural premium on egalitarian, personalistic skills in contrast to the impersonalistic modes of interaction suited to the

*Your energy*
*can tip the scales*
*when you add it*
*to thousands of others' –*
*merging,*
*slowly raising*
*our collective consciousness*
*to the point of power*
*when it makes*
*the all-important difference!*

*This survival energy spreads*
*far beyonds those involved*
*and touches every life*
*on Earth!*
– Ken Keyes, Jr,
*The Hundreth Monkey*

## DECIDE TO NETWORK

*Use every letter you write*
*Every conversation you have*
*Every meeting you attend*
*To express your fundamental*
*beliefs and dreams*
*Affirm to others the vision of*
*the world you want*
*Network through thought*
*Network through action*
*Network through love*
*Network through the spirit*
*You are the centre of a*
*network*
*You are the centre of the*
*world*
*You are a free, immensely*
*powerful source*
*of life and goodness*
*Affirm it*
*Spread it*
*Radiate it*
*Think day and night about*
*it*
*And you will see a miracle*
*happen:*
*the greatness of your own*
*life.*
*In a world of big powers,*
*media, and monopolies*
*But of four and a half billion*
*individuals*
*networking is the new*
*freedom*
*the new democracy*
*A new form of happiness.*
– Robert Muller

bureaucratic paradigm.'[52] New electronic forms of communication such as teleconferencing, computer modems and electronic mailings make it certain that networking will continue to play an important part in the activities of the rising counter culture.

Holistic change must, by definition, deal in wholes. Change cannot be conceived of as a compartmentalised, linear process, but rather as a process of dynamic interaction between all parties and interests involved. To try to change just one part of the system will send reverberations through the system which will eventually feed back and influence, perhaps adversely, whatever success was achieved in that one part. To achieve effective change it is, therefore, essential for the change agent or change agents to address the system as a whole. It is equally important for the change agent(s) to recognise that change is a multi-layered, multi-directional and multi-dimensional process. The impetus for change can come 'from the top', but change can also happen in a bottom-upwards or sideways direction. It can be triggered at one level just as much as another. Ideally, change involves real partnership and dialogue between all those involved. Change that is fragmentary or cosmetic is likely to meet with limited success, the change agents perhaps finding their own goals thwarted as their ideas are selectively taken on board to bolster the *status quo*. Schools, for instance, have been prepared to take on some features of holistic education – such as co-operative learning, community involvement and negotiated assessment – without necessarily adjusting their underlying purposes, values and worldview. In such cases, an important function of those sharing the new paradigm is to be alert to and assiduous in exposing the flaws and inconsistencies bred by such a 'shopping basket' approach to change.

From an holistic perspective, change must be both inner- and outer-directed; it must address the personal as well as the political. Holistic educators have been sharply criticised from a 'red' point of view for placing too much faith in personal consciousness-raising and conversion as agents of social change. 'Radical social change,' objects John Huckle, 'comes about through political struggle to redistribute economic and political power and change the basis of decision-making.' Green teachers, he continues, 'stress co-operation and new ethics but make little mention of politics, conflict and power.'[53] Whilst what Huckle says is, perhaps, fair comment on much that has been said and written in the name of green/holistic thinking, his criticism uses as its basis a personal-political polarity that is in fact alien to a truly holistic worldview. That worldview

requires of us that we see personal and political transformation as integrated, complementary parts of the change
process. To concern oneself exclusively with personal
change is a form of self-indulgence and self-deception; the
psyche is massaged, but at the cost of failing to live within
the meaning of the new worldview. To concern oneself
exclusively with political change is an equally hollow affair
in that any political success achieved is likely to founder as
it encounters resistances and misunderstandings from the
many who have not internalised what the change is about.
'With the holistic sense of spirituality,' writes Petra Kelly,
'one's personal life is truly political and one's political life
is truly personal. Anyone who does not comprehend within
him- or herself this essential unity cannot achieve political
change on a deep level and cannot strive for the ideals of
the Greens.'[54]

---

*The character structure of the average individual and the
socioeconomic structure of the society of which he or she
is a part are interdependent. The relation between social
character and social structure is never static, since both
elements in this relationship are never-ending processes.
A change in either factor means a change in both. Many
political revolutionaries believe that one must first change
the political and economic structure radically, and that
then, as a second and almost necessary step, the human
mind will also change: that the new society, once
established, will quasiautomatically produce the new
human being. They do not see that the new elite, being
motivated by the same character as the old one, will tend
to recreate the conditions of the old society in the new
sociopolitical institutions the revolution has created; that
the victory of the revolution will be its defeat as a
revolution – although not as an historical phase that paved
the way for the socioeconomic development that was
hobbled in its full development. The French and Russian
revolutions are textbook examples. On the other side are
those who claim that first the nature of human beings
must change – their consciousness, their values, their
character – and that only then can a truly human society
be built. The history of the human race proves them
wrong. Purely physical change has always remained in
the private sphere and been restricted to small oases, or
has been completely ineffective when the preaching of
spiritual values was combined with the practice of the
opposite values.*

– Erich Fromm, *To Have or to Be?*

---

## You Tides with Ceaseless Swell

You tides with ceaseless swell! you power that does this work!
You unseen force, centripetal, centrifugal, through space's spread,
Rapport of sun, moon, earth, and all the constellations,
What are the messages by you from distant stars to us? what Sirius'? What Capella's?
What central heart – and you the pulse – vivifies all? what boundless aggregate of all?
What subtle indirection and significance in you? what clue to all in you? what fluid, vast identity,
Holding the universe with all its parts as one – as sailing in a ship?

– Walt Whitman

An holistic view of change, in short, moves the goal posts. Denying old polarities and free of the reductionism and divisiveness implicit in all ideologies, it allows us to see change afresh; the bubble loses its opaqueness. Taking as their starting point the view that the fragmentationalist worldview is outdated, that it will be inevitably discarded as people come to recognise its mismatch with reality, its adherents recall John Maynard Keynes' exhortation that 'the power of vested interests is vastly exaggerated compared with the gradual encroachment of ideas.'[55]

# Changing Schools

The education system has not been left unaffected by the emergence of the holistic worldview; there are new paradigm 'conspirators' in schools just as there are in all walks of life. Enough developments and initiatives have taken place in schools in recent years to signal that the old is being challenged by the new. In curriculum terms we have seen the inclusion of development, environmental, human rights and peace perspectives in courses offered in many schools; perspectives that emphasise the personal as well as the political; that emphasise the exploration of values and attitudes and the development of social and political skills as much as the accumulation of facts. In methodological terms, we have witnessed a fairly widespread diversification in learning styles to cater for different learning needs. In particular, this has involved a shift away from frontal teaching and individualised narrow academic learning towards interactive, participatory and co-operative learning strategies. In organisational and structural terms, we have seen some examples of devolution of power by the school executive to the teaching staff as a whole, in some cases incorporating a (perhaps tokenistic) recognition of students' rights to participation in the decision-making process. Some schools have also become more open to the community through imaginative community education programmes and all schools have become more responsive to parents as a result of recent legislative reforms. These developments notwithstanding, schools do not, in their overall working and organisation, reflect an holistic worldview; they are still, by and large, engine houses of fragmentationalism.

Douglas Ogilvie argues that schools, like other organisations, will inevitably espouse more holistic working styles; that it is natural for human organisations 'to progress from the mechanistic to the organic form, in spite of current inhibitions'. The organic organisation, he argues, can be differentiated from the mechanistic organisation in terms of its structure, policy making and initiation of change, purpose, forms of control and communication, and membership. The structure of the mechanistic organisation is marked by an authoritarian hierarchy and discrete horizontal status divisions 'with high status individuals in the performance of specific tasks'. The structure of the organic organisation, on the other hand, is 'formed of flexible, overlapping situs groupings' with responsibility for a particular activity and to which individuals can attach themselves. To improve its performance, a 'situs grouping' may delegate outwards but in no sense is their delegation downards (or upwards) to those of a lower (or higher) status. Policy decision-making in mechanistic organisations is decided upon by 'privileged controllers', whereas in organic organisations policy is determined consensually. 'Any individual member or situs in an organic organisation is considered free to initiate acts of leadership which are followed by fellow-members if deemed by them to be appropriate.' This contrasts with the mechanistic system wherein designated heads or directors are held responsible for initiating change and innovation. 'It is largely because of this difference that organic organisations are more innovative, flexible, creative and lively, while mechanistic organisations are more predictable, inflexible, reproductive and lifeless.' The prime purpose for a mechanistic organisation is collective, in the strictly institutional sense, with its members often sublimating their real needs for material reward or promotion. Organic organisations seek to 'facilitate the expression of the individual uniqueness of all members'. The focus is on the present quality of life within the institution (processes, communications, relationships) as against working towards a product. Control in mechanistic organisations is vested in authority figures (that authority normally flowing from their position but sometimes from their personality) whilst organic control derives from a sense of shared commitment and responsibility and from egalitarian consensus. The nature of control in mechanistic organisations tends to create factionalism and inhibited, secretive and hypocritical forms of communication with an emphasis on impersonal interaction. Collegial democracy in organic organisations needs and prioritises 'open, honest, caring, uninhibited communication of both rational thought and emotional feeling'. It works on 'communication networks and decoding mechanisms that are equally accessible to all members'. The membership of an organic organisation is likely to be made up of 'mature human beings' able to integrate their reason and intellect with their emotions, instincts and intuitions. The ethos of a mechanistic organisation, on the other hand, promotes the denial of maturity.[56]

## Features of Mechanistic and Organic Organisations

| Dimensions of Difference | Mechanistic Organisations | Organic Organisations |
|---|---|---|
| Structure | Hierarchy; unequal status; delegation downwards (or upwards) | Heterarchy; equal status; delegation outwards |
| Policy making/change initiation | By authority; restricted number of sources of change | Consensual; change initiated from anywhere within the organisation |
| Purpose | Collective (involving sacrifice of personal needs and potentials); extrinsic satisfactions through product orientation | Expressive of individual needs and potentials; intrinsic satisfactions through person/process orientation |
| Control | Flowing from authority figures | Shared, consensual |
| Communication | Inhibited, closed and factional | Uninhibited, open and communal |
| Membership | Social and mental adolescents | Social and mental adults |

After Ogilvie, D., 'The organisational alternatives' in Dufty, D., & H., eds., *Thinking Whole. The quest for a new educational paradigm*, Social Education Association of Australia, 1988, 107.

'It is the responsibility of genuine educators,' concludes Ogilvie, 'to promote the personal development of people (particularly themselves) to the mental maturity wherein the crucial choice can be faced between retaining the mechanistic form and experimenting with the organic form. Adults (who accept the drive for personal freedom and communal love as the essential characteristic of the human being) might then be expected to insist on the organic form of organisation as a natural human right, rather than dismissing it as a pie-in-the-sky dream. Such people, by acting as if they are members of organic organisations, could transform those organisations (and themselves) from the inside in a quiet revolution. Such organisational (and personal) development would be a natural, reasonable and emergent process, rather than the artificial, authoritarian and imposed manipulation that is promoted by so much of the institutionalised literature on "organisational development" and "personal development".'[57]

Schools are changing and will continue to change as we break out of the conceptual bubble of fragmentationalism. The thrust of opinion amongst those espousing the holistic worldview is that we can all help change along; that even in the most unlikely context there are things that can be done. The main part of this book is given over to reviewing how teachers and others involved in education have gone about effecting change so that our schools can better set about educating whole people for a whole planet. First, however, we examine the extent to which the holistic view of change, as discussed in this chapter, marries with the thinking of those professionally involved in analysing change processes in schools.

We must learn to focus easily and lovingly our minds, hearts, senses and souls over the entire gamut of creation, from the infinitely large to the infinitely small, from the stars to the flowers of the earth, from the entire human family to the last of our sisters and bretheren, embracing at any moment the plenitude of the miracle of creation and of being.

Infinitely more attention must be accorded to the great, simple and so effective concepts of love, peace, compassion, truth, purity, goodness, humility, faith, divinity, the heart, the soul, resurrection, infinity and eternity. They must become the luminous pillars of human civilization in a global, universal context.

– Robert Muller

BBC/North South Productions

# References

1. Schwarz, D., & W., 'The Whole Truth', *The Guardian*, 15.7.87, 11.

2. Capra, F., *The Tao of Physics*, Flamingo, 1983, 28.

3. Bateson, G., *Steps to an Ecology of Mind*, Granada, 1973, 436.

4. Smith, H., 'Beyond the Modern Western Mind Set', in Sloan, D., ed., *Towards the Recovery of Wholeness. Knowledge, Education and Human Values*, New York, Teachers College Press, Columbia University, 1981, 68.

5. Briggs, J. P., & Peat, F. D., *Looking Glass Universe. The Emerging Science of Wholeness*, Fontana, 1985, 33.

6. See, for instance, Capra, F., *op. cit.* and Zukav, G., *The Dancing Wu Li Masters*, Bantam, 1986.

7. Bohm, D., 'The Implicate and the Super-implicate Order', in Weber, R., *Dialogues with Scientists and Sages: the Search for Unity*, Routledge & Kegan Paul, 1986, 23–49.

8. *Ibid.*, 30.

9. *Ibid.*, 30–1 (see, also, Bohm, D., *Wholeness and the Implicate Order*, Routledge & Kegan Paul, 1980).

10. *Ibid.*, 44.

11. Sloan, D., ed., *op. cit.*, 2; see also Bohm's essay, 'Insight, Knowledge, Science and Human Values', in the same work, 8–30.

12. Porritt, J., & Winner, D., *The Coming of the Greens*, Fontana, 1988, 234.

13. See, for instance, Roszak, T., *Person/Planet*, Granada, 1978, 4, 26.

14. Pietroni, P., *Holistic Living. A Guide to Self-care by a Leading Practitioner*, Dent, 1986, 169–71.

15. Smith, H., *op. cit.*, 66.

16. See, for instance, Illich, I., *Celebration of Awareness*, Calder & Boyars, 1971.

17. Higgins, R., *The Seventh Enemy. The Human Factor in the Global Crisis*, Pan, 1980, 240.

18. Robertson, J., *The Sane Alternative*, James Robertson, Spring Cottage, 9 New Road, Ironbridge, Shropshire TF8 7AU, 1983, 23.

19. *Ibid.*, 22–8.

20. Higgins, R., *op. cit.*, 240–5; see also, Porritt, J., *Seeing Green, The Politics of Ecology Explained*, Basil Blackwell, 1984, 200–3; and Leland, S., 'Feminism and ecology: theoretical connections', in Caldecott, L., & Leland, S., eds., *Reclaim the Earth. Women Speak Out for Life on Earth*, The Women's Press, 1983, 71.

21. Bowen, M., 'The Ecology of Knowledge: Linking the Natural and Social Sciences', in Dufty, D., & H., eds., *Thinking Whole, The Quest for a New Educational Paradigm*, Sydney, Social Education Association of Australia, 1988, 90–1.

22. Virginia Cawagas used this phrase when she spoke to 'The Turning Point' Conference held at the University of Sydney, Australia, from 12 to 16 January 1988.

23. Porritt, J., *op. cit.*, 200.

24. Capra, F., *op. cit.*, 99–101.

25. Bateson, G., *op. cit.*, 436–42.

26. Lovelock, J. E., *Gaia. A New Look at Life on Earth*, Oxford University Press, 1982, 145.

27. Russell, P., *The Awakening Earth. Our Next Evolutionary Leap*, Routledge & Kegan Paul, 1982, 183.

28. Porritt, J., *op. cit.*, 208.

29. *Ibid*, 222.

30. Cited in Gerber, A., 'Towards a Holistic Paradigm for Education. A Communication Approach', in Dufty, D., & H., *op. cit.*, 121.

31. Rifkin, J., *Entropy. A New World View*, Paladin, 1985, 249.

32. Bohm, D., in Sloan, D., *op. cit.*, 25.

33. Rifkin, J., *op. cit.*, 249.

34. Bohm, D., in Weber, R., *op. cit.*, 37.

35. Spretnak, C., 'Ten Key Values of the American Green Movement', *Green Teacher*, 6, December, 1987, 25.

36. For a discussion of global and futures education, see Pike, G., & Selby, D. E., *Global Teacher, Global Learner*, Hodder & Stoughton, 1988.

37. This quote by John Tideman is cited in Dufty, D., & H., eds., *'The Turning Point' Conference. Looking Forward, Looking Back*, Sydney, Social Education Association of Australia, 1988, 22.

38. Sloan, D., *op. cit.*, 6.

39. Odou, N., cited in Dufty, D. & H., eds., *Thinking Whole*, Sydney, Social Education Association of Australia, 1988, 23.

40. On centering, see Hendricks, G., *The Centered Teacher*, New Jersey, Prentice-Hall, 1981; Hendricks, G., & Wills, R., *The Centering Book*, New Jersey, Prentice-Hall, 1975; Hendricks, G., & Roberts, T. B., *The Second Centering Book*, New Jersey, Prentice-Hall, 1977.

41. Sloan, D., *op. cit.*, 5.

42. *Ibid.*

43. Ferguson, M., *The Aquarian Conspiracy*, Granada, 1980, 76.

44. Gough, N., 'Learning with Environments . . . An Ecological Paradigm for Education', *Green Teacher*, 8 March 1988, 13.

45. *Ibid.*, 15.

46. Dufty, D., & H., eds., *'The Turning Point' Conference. Looking Forward Looking Back*, Sydney, Social Education Association of Australia, 1988, 9.

47. Capra, F., *The Turning Point. Science, Society and the Rising Culture*, Flamingo, 1983, 6–30.

48. Ferguson, M., *op. cit.*, 26.

49. Porritt, J., & Winner, D., *op. cit.*, 15–16;

50. Capra, F., *op. cit.*, 15.

51. Ferguson, M., *op. cit.*, 36.

52. Hine, V. H., 'The Basic Paradigm of a Future Socio-cultural System', *World Issues*, April/May 1977, 19, cited in Elgin, D., *Voluntary Simplicity*, New York, William Morrow, 1981, 292.

53. Huckle, J., 'Ten Red Questions to Ask Green Teachers', *Green Teacher*, 2, December 1986, 13.

54. Spretnak, C., & Capra, F., *Green Politics. The Global Promise*, Paladin, 1985, 52.

55. Cited in Porritt, J., *op. cit.*, 198.

56. Ogilvie, D., *The Organisational Alternatives*, in Dufty, D., & H., eds., *Thinking Whole*, Sydney, Social Education Association of Australia, 1988, 105–10.

57. *Ibid.*, 109–10.

·CHAPTER TWO·

# From Green Papers to Green Schools: Some Theories of Change

## The failure of 'blueprints for change'

It is certainly no coincidence that one of the most significant achievements of scientific endeavour based on a fragmentationalist worldview – the launching of Sputnik I by
the Soviet Union – should trigger the modern era of
planned change in schools. In response to the perceived
deficiencies in science education in US schools, the
National Science Foundation launched several large-scale
curriculum projects, whilst in the UK similar ventures in
maths, science and modern languages were sponsored by
the Nuffield Foundation. The Research, Development and
Diffusion (R, D & D) model of curriculum development
which shaped these projects had impeccable credentials
amongst the scientific community. Change would come
about, it was thought, as a rational outcome of providing
new classroom materials which had been carefully prepared
by experts and extensively trialled in schools. During the
relative prosperity of the 1960s, large sums of money were
invested by the Department of Education and Science in
setting up the first generation of Schools Council projects,
based on a similar model and with high hopes of fundamentally influencing the curriculum. Such expectations
were rarely fulfilled. The DES itself judged the Schools
Council's performance as 'generally mediocre'[1], whilst the
Impact and Take-up project, reporting on its 1978 survey
of secondary schools, stated that 'the majority of (Schools)
Council-funded projects providing teaching materials were
used by less than 10 per cent of the relevant teachers.'[2]

> *What a strange machine man
> is! You fill him with bread,
> wine, fish and radishes, and
> out of him come sighs,
> laughter and dreams.*
>
> – Nikos Kazantzakis,
> *Zorba the Greek*

A major problem with the R, D & D model, it seemed, was the *Diffusion* stage. The dissemination of new materials into schools did not necessarily prompt their use in the classroom: teachers, unlike microchips, do not automatically behave according to a predetermined programme. The basic weakness of the model was recognised in the construction of some later Schools Council projects, such as the Humanities Curriculum Project and the Industry Project. The fact that such projects were not locked into a specific subject area was significant in that it caused the project teams to think seriously about the target audience, which in turn brought consideration of change strategies and models to the forefront of curriculum development.[3] A principal tenet of the emerging strategy was collaboration, based on the view, prevalent in the Schools Council by about 1970, 'that it was involvement in the process (by the teachers) rather than reception of the materials which was the significant thing about curriculum development.'[4] Involving teachers in the process required the participation, too, of local authority advisers, teachers' centre wardens and teacher trainers in a working partnership which focussed as much on professional development as on the production of materials.

From an early emphasis on change as product, the process of change became a major consideration for curriculum developers in the late 1970s. Coincidentally, this period witnessed the closing down of many national curriculum projects in England and Wales, and the beginning of a time of considerable financial retrenchment in education. For these reasons the focus of innovation had shifted, by the early 1980s, away from centralised projects towards school-based curriculum development; a process of change which could identify local needs and priorities and respond spontaneously to new trends. In such a move can be seen a recognition of the school as part of a wider community and social system and of the need to consider the environment of the classroom as critical for the initiation of change, as well as for its dissemination. School-based curriculum development, a 'bottom-upwards' approach, represents a fundamental critique of the 'top-downwards' R, D & D model. It is also a reflection, some argue, of 'those movements in contemporary culture which give prominence to activism by small groups, the questioning of traditional hierarchies, and the substitution of the critical processes of inquiry and valuation for those of assimilation and value acceptance.'[5] The shift away from fragmentationalist thinking, from devising 'blueprints for change', is to be welcomed though it still lacks, as we shall argue later, a clear understanding of how change occurs within a system. More worrying, however, is the recent thrust of educational policy in the UK towards centralisation, not simply of innovation in schools, but of control of the curriculum itself (see Chapter 7).

This potted history of curriculum development cannot, of course, do justice to the wealth of initiatives – at national, regional and local levels – which have influenced teachers' thinking and practice during the last thirty years. It is impossible to evaluate just how much impact a particular project, in-service workshop or set of materials has made on classroom practice, though the chapters that follow give some evidence of highly innovative and creative change processes in operation. Much research on educational change, however, clearly indicates that such creative class-room practice is not the norm, despite the considerable investment in curriculum and professional development summarised above. The central aims of this chapter are to identify the pitfalls and shortcomings of previous attempts at educational change and then to propose a model of change which both reflects and promotes 'a greening of education'.

## The meaning of change

Two major strands of criticism emerge from assessments of innovation in education. The first is that many designs for change fail to take sufficient account of what Seymour Sarason calls 'the culture of the school'.[6] The second, and related, strand concerns the lack of consideration given to ensure that those centrally involved in change processes – principally teachers – understand, in Michael Fullan's term, the 'meaning of educational change'.[7] The culture of the school and its implications for change will be explored in the next section; let us now try to establish what innovation means for many teachers.

*'If any one of them can explain it,' said Alice, 'I'll give him sixpence. I don't believe there's an atom of meaning in it.' 'If there's no meaning in it,' said the King, 'that saves a world of trouble, you know, as we needn't try to find any.'*
*– Lewis Carroll,*
*Alice in Wonderland*

A truism, significant for the regularity with which it seems to be overlooked, is that the perception of change held by the designer or instigator is likely to be somewhat different from that of the recipient. From his experience of evaluating Schools Council projects, Carl Parsons discerns a significant gulf between the 'educationist orientation', and the 'practitioner perspective'.[8] This 'gap between worlds' lies at the heart of many problems in educational change. The underpinning philosophy of much curriculum and professional development is rooted in the world of the educationist: a set of values and assumptions about the nature and direction of education which are hewn within the walls of universities and colleges and henceforth employed in Department of Education and Science Green Papers, policy statements from County Hall and in-service courses at teachers' centres. The guiding philosophy of much classroom practice is altogether more pragmatic and utilitarian, concerned largely with the daunting demands of 'custodialism and certification'.[9] The 'gap between worlds', however, cannot of itself be blamed for the failure of attempts to introduce new ideas and practices into the classroom. There are many striking examples, in this book and elsewhere, of seasoned classroom practitioners successfully and faithfully implementing lofty ideals dreamt up at an ivory-towered distance. Indeed, it could be argued that a difference in perspective is necessary for creative growth in education; that the vision of the educationist is to broaden the blinkered reality of the classroom, not to become blinded by it. The crux of the matter concerns the relationship between the educationist and the practitioner, change agent and recipient of change. As Peter Marris explains:

> *When those who have power to manipulate change act as if they have only to explain, and when their explanations are not at once accepted, shrug off opposition as ignorance or prejudice, they express a profound contempt for the meaning of lives other than their own. For the reformers have already assimilated these changes to their purposes . . . If they deny others the chance to do the same, they treat them as puppets dangling by the threads of their own conceptions.[10]*

*When the forms of an old culture are dying, the new culture is created by a few people who are not afraid to be insecure.*

– Rudolf Bahro

Change in schools, if it is to be successful, must have meaning for teachers, for whom it is not simply a question of accepting a new product, but of embarking on a learning process. There is a critical disharmony between medium and message in so much educational change: educationists and administrators who promote change treat teachers in the same way as they have previously criticised teachers for treating students.[11] It is perversely ironic when calls for teachers to be more sensitive to students' needs are made in a manner which is insensitive to teachers' needs. The cause of this disharmony, contends Michael Fullan, is the failure to distinguish between *change* and *the change process*. This is exemplified in the idea, prevalent in many Schools Council projects, that involving *some* practising teachers in curriculum development would smooth the way for the implementation of new ideas and practice because it would increase acceptance by *other* teachers.[12] Change, however, is a highly personal experience which does not readily subscribe to such logic. All real change involves 'passing through the zones of uncertainty . . . the situation of being at sea, of being lost, of confronting more infor-

Every atom in this body existed before organic life emerged 4000 million years ago. Remember our childhood as minerals, as lava, as rocks? Rocks contain the potentiality to weave themselves into such stuff as this. We are the rocks dancing. Why do we look down on them with such a condescending air? It is they that are the immortal part of us.

– John Seed, *Thinking like a Mountain*

Simon Warner

*Only connect!*

– E. M. Forster. Epigraph to
*Howards End*

*Thinking means connecting
things, and stops if they
cannot be connected.*

– G. K. Chesterton

mation than you can handle.'[13] The fact that other colleagues may have been involved in the development of a new curriculum will be of little comfort to the teacher who is struggling to get to grips with unfamiliar methods and materials in the isolation of her classroom.

A teacher's inability to understand a process of change, a failure to find meaning, is a classic symptom of fragmentationalist thinking in education. Such thinking regards the teacher as a machine which, once programmed, will operate in the required manner; it distances and objectifies the relationship between the educationist and the practitioner; and it fails to recognise the crucial learning process which must take place if the goal of change is to be achieved. Blueprints for change can, of course, have partial success. National science projects are likely to produce some more able scientists; policies on anti-racist education may lead to an increase in tolerance between different ethnic groups and promote greater equality (though the available evidence in the UK tends to question this). Central to the purpose of this book, however, is the suggestion that the maximisation of effort towards change in schools will only come about with a clearer understanding of the interrelationship of all elements in the change process. As with the girl blowing bubbles, meaning is derived from connectedness.

## The culture of the school

It has been suggested that many large-scale curriculum development projects in Britain and the United States failed to have much impact in the classroom because of insufficient understanding of the culture of the school. Educational reformers, it seems, were not connected to the everyday realities of teachers. One of the great conundrums facing the teacher is that she is expected to work, for most of the day, in a densely populated environment but in psychological isolation. In his wide-ranging research on what US teachers do and think, Dan Lortie found that a sense of isolation was a predominant feeling; teachers tended to wrestle with their anxieties and problems privately, and nearly half of those surveyed reported having 'no contact' with colleagues in carrying out their work. Another common characteristic of teachers' psychological state, Lortie found, was uncertainty. They were not sure whether they could make all students learn; they were uncertain where their influence began and ended, or whether they had made any impact at all. Assessment of their own performance was, therefore, highly problematic.[14] Taking a broader view, Huberman summarises the everyday reality of the classroom under three dimensions:

> **multi-dimensionality**: the classroom as a crowded place with several activities and functions to be carried out;
> **simultaneity**: interacting with one student and monitoring others, preparing the next question or exercise, directing simultaneous groups, etc;
> **unpredictability**; anything can happen: a well-planned lesson may fall flat, what works with one child is ineffective with another, one feels one's way through the day, etc. [15]

Multi-dimensional, simultaneous, unpredictable . . . the classroom as a system, a ceaseless flow of energy, matter, ideas and information all in constant interaction and change. Enter the educational reform: objective, precise, planned, gleaming with moral certainty. Like the meeting of two alien cultures, the resultant interaction abounds with suspicion, anxiety, misunderstanding and retrenchment.

Most teachers, argues Michael Fullan, are not against change *per se*, but they do not like the way in which change is introduced. [16] In their assessment of any given or proposed change, teachers commonly employ 'the practicality ethic'. It comprises three main criteria:

1. Does the change potentially address a need? Will students be interested? Will they learn?
2. How clear is the change in terms of what the teacher will have to do?
3. How will it affect the teacher personally in terms of time, energy, new skill, sense of excitement and competence, and interference with existing priorities? [17]

It is interesting to reflect that, whilst the target of most educational reform is the student, two out of the three assessment criteria employed by teachers focus on themselves. Born out of the pervasive sense of isolation and uncertainty, teachers cry out for new ideas, methods and materials which will help them to make sense of their world. It would be tempting to conclude from this analysis that all innovations for the classroom should consist solely of practical 'tips for teachers' which can facilitate their many professional tasks without adding to their burden. Whilst the appeal of 'classroom goodies' should not be underestimated, such a conclusion again confuses change as product and change as process. Elliott's research into how teachers learn suggests that practice has an important role to play in the acquisition of new theory, namely that 'theoretical knowledge contributes to the learning of a skill

> *We have oversold the benefits of technology and external manipulations; we have undersold the importance of human relationships and the complexity of nature.*
>
> – Marilyn Ferguson

only after a certain level of practical knowledge has first been acquired.'[18] Practice, then, is a crucial element in the learning process of change.

It should come as no surprise, given the subjective reality of the classroom, that many grand designs for change fail, or at best, only partially succeed. Common outcomes of attempts at innovation are two forms of non-change: *false clarity*, when teachers think that change has occurred but, in actuality, only the superficial trappings of a new practice have been assimilated; and *painful unclarity*, an experience derived from an unclear innovation which fails to address the teacher's need to find meaning in change.[19] Most educationists can probably identify with the first, and most teachers with the second; both are frustrating experiences. But in spite of this pessimistic outlook – despite, perhaps, planned attempts at innovation in education – any historical overview will indicate that change *has* occurred in schools, for better or worse. Curricula have been updated to include new knowledge and understanding; skills more relevant to the late twentieth century have become part of the school diet; values and attitudes – probably the area most resistant to change – have fluctuated according to the prevailing moral, social and political climate. In the light of evidence pointing to non-change, one might well ask: how has this happened? There are, of course, differences in degree and scale: the impact of one project cannot be justly compared with a national trend. But that is only part of the answer. Another part can be identified from a more holistic view of change: a view which sees the culture of the classroom and of the school in constant interaction with the wider culture of the community, the society, the planet; a view of change as a natural, organic process which, if we allow it, encompasses and involves us all. We shall explore this further in the next section. Another explanation for change is often concealed on account of the limitations of sociological surveys. They paint a picture of common practice by tending to obscure that which deviates from the norm; as the interviews and case studies in this book amply demonstrate, not *all* teachers are isolated, bewildered and suspicious of change.

It seems probable that teachers' attitudes towards change in education are related to the underlying values and assumptions of their teaching. John Miller provides a clear exposition of these in his identification of three basic positions of curriculum and instruction: *transmission*, *transaction* and *transformation*.[20] Using this framework one might postulate upon key elements of the underlying worldviews and attendant theories of change. (See opposite).

| curriculum and instruction position | worldview | theory of change |
|---|---|---|
| *transmission:* | *fragmentalism:* | *traditionalism/ conservatism:* |
| education is a one-way, top-downward movement of certain knowledge, skills and values; its focus is the traditional school subject taught in a traditional way; the student is seen as a passive recipient of conveniently packaged and programmed blocks of teaching. | humankind is divorced from nature and can therefore exploit the environment; nature is made up of a series of isolated building blocks; individuals are encouraged to compete in the market-place, as free agents. | traditions must be maintained – change needs to be checked and controlled; parts of a system can be changed if they do not work effectively; social change comes about through the efforts of successful individuals. |
| *transaction:* | *pragmatism:* | *intervention:* |
| education is a dialogue between the student and the curriculum; the focus is on teaching strategies which facilitate problem-solving; the student is seen as rational and capable of solving problems, if given the right tools. | humankind can improve the environment through the use of rational planning; science and technology can solve the problems the planet faces; individual behaviour is predictable and can be monitored through legislation. | change needs to be introduced and managed in a rational and scientific manner; social improvement requires deliberate intervention by some individuals for the good of others. |
| *transformation:* | *holism:* | *organicism:* |
| education is a process of personal and social development; it focusses on the aesthetic, moral, physical and spiritual needs of the student as well as her cognitive attainment; the student is viewed as a whole person. | all life on the planet is interconnected and interdependent; meaning is derived from understanding relationships; individuals cannot act in isolation – the actions of any one impact on the system. | change is an inevitable and natural function of a system; change only has meaning in the context of the system; social improvement comes about through dismantling the human-made barriers to change. |

Most attempts at educational change over the last thirty years would seem to fall clearly within the interventionist mode: through rational planning and action, many problems in schools can be solved. Teachers who adopt a predominantly *transactionist* position in their teaching are most likely to react positively towards this process of innovation and be able to identify with and find meaning in its basic goals and assumptions. Many teachers, however, operate from a *transmission* position; their conservative attitude towards change is likely to induce resistance to the need for innovation and rejection of the interventionist process. For the *transformationist* teacher, such rational planning is likely to be viewed as yet another crass, bureaucratic intrusion upon the development of the student as a whole person. Not only does the 'culture of the school' and 'the culture of the classroom' need to be taken into account in the change process, but also 'the culture of the person': the underlying values, perspectives and assumptions which formulate a teacher's worldview and determine her beliefs and behaviour in relation to education and to change. 'We need to take a whole life perspective,' argues Peter Woods on the basis of research on the impact of teachers' self-development in formulating attitudes to the curriculum. 'Our data have suggested how the formulation of self in early years may relate to later teaching and handling of a subject area, and the part played in the formulation of that self by such factors as home environment, parents, teachers, marriage and socio-economic and political factors. We need to give more consideration to this whole life perspective . . . if we are to do the study of the curriculum – and the people involved in it – full justice.'[21]

> *For men and women are not only themselves: they are also the region in which they were born, the city apartment or farm in which they learned to walk, the games they played as children, the old wives' tales they overheard, the food they ate, the schools they attended, the sports they followed, the poems they read, and the God they believed in.*
>
> – W. Somerset Maugham, *The Razor's Edge*

## Beyond the management of change

In a recent seminar at the National Foundation for Educational Research,[22] Michael Fullan – perhaps the most influential writer of the decade on educational change – suggested that research and writing about innovation in schools indicated three phases. Phase one, up to about 1978, was *failure*: a catalogue of case studies documenting the lack of take-up of new ideas, methods and materials. Phase two, up to the mid-1980s, was *success*: research highlighted effective schools and teachers, and provided case studies of innovation that worked. Phase three, the present, he characterised as the *management of change*: research concentrated upon guidelines and techniques for achieving change in schools. To a large extent the models of educational change in the UK outlined at the beginning of this chapter illustrate these three phases. The R, D & D model, with its orientation towards change as product, failed to bring about much change; the collaborative approach, involving teachers and others in all phases of a project, was rather more successful; whilst the focus on school-based curriculum development was beginning to highlight the importance of understanding the process of change in the context of the culture of the school.

---

*In the pursuit of learning, every day something is acquired.*
*In the pursuit of Tao, every day something is dropped.*

*Less and less is done*
*Until non-action is achieved.*
*When nothing is done, nothing is left undone.*

*The world is ruled by letting things take their course.*
*It cannot be ruled by interfering.*

*– Lao Tsu*

---

Within the term 'management of change', however, can be detected the strains of fragmentationalist thinking. Whilst accepting that this view of change has gone a long way towards understanding the complexities of the school as a system, implicit in the concept of 'management' is the idea of change being initiated, shaped and guided by a group of trained experts for the benefit of others. It is a form of rational intervention, solving the problem of a part of the system which appears to be malfunctioning. An holistic view of the world regards change as a natural, organic process; by the very nature of a system, in which everything is in constant and dynamic interaction with everything else, change is inevitable. In ancient Chinese philosophy, Tao – the Way – is the process of ceaseless motion and activity which is the essence of the universe. A state of immobility or passivity is thus inconceivable, even though the term *wu wei*, frequently used in Taoist philosophy, means literally 'non-action'. According to Chuang

Tzu: 'Non-action does not mean doing nothing and keeping silent. Let everything be allowed to do what it naturally does, so that its nature will be satisfied.'[23] Activity falls into two kinds: activity which is in harmony with nature and activity against the natural flow of things.[24] Change that results from the former kind might be called *organic change*.

In schools, as in every other social institution, organic change is potentially omnipresent. The extent to which it occurs, however, depends upon how much human activity is of the first rather than of the second kind; in other words, upon *how much it is allowed to happen*. The teacher who adopts a transmission position in the classroom severely limits the potential for organic change through fragmenting the curriculum and reducing students to passive objects. The transactionist teacher also restricts organic change through over-emphasising cognitive development and problem-solving: many problems faced by students are not finally soluble through rational analysis alone. By focussing on the development of the whole person, the transformationist teacher facilitates the process of organic change, encouraging students to see the connectedness of themselves to each other and to their environment.

> *All conservatism is based upon the idea that if you leave things alone you leave them as they are. But you do not. If you have a thing alone you leave it to a torrent of change.*
> – G. K. Chesterton

If change is a natural process, then we – educationists who want to see change in schools – do not need to do anything. That would be a rational conclusion to be drawn from the above theory. It presupposes, however, that the system in which we want change to happen is itself a natural legalitarian one, which is clearly not the case. Schools have, for a long time, operated on the basis of fragmentationist thought and action. The major task, then, for the educationist who wishes to facilitate organic change in schools is that of removing the age-old, encrusted barriers to change, the most pervasive of these being the fragmentationist mindset itself. Let us not underestimate the enormity and complexity of this task, the need for courage, commitment and constant self-criticism. For it is probable that we are in a position to facilitate change because we are advantaged by a fragmentationist approach. Truly organic change will only materialise with the lifting of the oppressive burdens which stifle the creative spirits and voices of marginalised groups in our society; groups which, on account of their race, gender, handicap, class or cultural background, are not permitted to contribute to the process of change. 'It is deeply alarming,' contends Robin Richardson, 'and *prima facie* very significant, that most of the main literature on curriculum development and reform and on school improvement and organisational development, has made no reference at all, or at best no more than passing ritualistic reference, to racism and racial injustice in schools.'[25] Our capacity as educational reformers for barrier removal may be vital, but so too is our humility, a willingness to encourage and encompass all natural forces for change and to allow ourselves to be changed by them.

We suggested earlier that an understanding of connectedness between all elements of the change process was vital for establishing meaning. In organic change, relationship is everything. Just as the yellowing leaf of an oak tree does not make sense outside an appreciation of the tree's connectedness to the natural seasons, so a change in the curriculum needs to be seen in the broad context of the school, the community and the wider world. It is certain that an intricate web of influences have nurtured and shaped any curriculum change, from prevailing social, economic and cultural trends to the individual experiences and perspectives of a teacher and her students. Let us consider the introduction of a new Integrated Humanities syllabus. The need for a new syllabus will probably have arisen because of new perceptions concerning the goals, methods and materials of humanities teaching. Such perceptions are likely to be integral to wider educational thinking and practice, which in turn will be linked to social and political pressures and preoccupations, such as the needs of industry, citizenship or a new morality. The designers of the new syllabus – a collaborative working group of teachers, academics and educationists – will bring, individually and collectively, a multitude of assumptions, values and ideals which will underpin their contributions. The finished product is thus much more than a statement of the necessary knowledge, skills and attitudes for students of humanities to acquire; it represents a *mélange* of contemporary thought and feeling, channelled into a seemingly objective syllabus. At every twist and turn of the dissemination phase of this innovation, the new product is subject to myriad interpretations and influences. At in-service workshops and departmental meetings, it becomes more than just the product of the design team. In individual classrooms, the syllabus is exposed yet again to subtle modulation: the institutional constraints of time and resources; the personal convictions and characteristics of the teacher; the abilities and expectations of students; the impact of contemporaneous local, national and global events on school life, and so on. All of these factors will collectively determine the outcome of this particular curriculum change, and it cannot be finally understood without an appreciation of the multi-layered, multi-dimensional nature of the change process.

> *The unleashed power of the atom has changed everything except our way of thinking.*
> – Albert Einstein

> *To be sure of hitting the target, shoot first and, whatever you hit, call it the target.*
> – Ashleigh Brilliant

*Every ripple on the ocean*
*Every leaf on every tree*
*Every sand dune in the*
*desert*
*Every power we never see*
*There is a deeper wave than*
*this*
*Swelling in the world*
*There is a deeper wave than*
*this*
*Listen to me girl*

*Feel it rising in the cities*
*Feel it sweeping over land*
*Over borders, over frontiers*
*Nothing will its power*
*withstand*
*There is a deeper wave than*
*this*
*Rising in the world*
*There is a deeper wave than*
*this*
*Listen to me girl*

*I say love is the seventh wave*
*– Sting*

Faced with the goal of changing the curriculum, the rational planner makes laws, structures and predictions; the facilitator of organic change makes connections. The culture of the school, now recognized as crucial to any understanding of change, is but one part of a wider culture – a system within a system. An influential force within that larger system is what might be called the *zeitgeist*, the collective mood and aspirations of diverse social groups, a change-oriented set of values which infuse the beliefs and actions of a significant number of people and so bring about organic change. A prevailing *zeitgeist*, the 'Aquarian conspiracy' to use Marilyn Ferguson's term, represents the dissatisfaction felt by so many with the predominant, Western view of the world derived from the fragmentationalist thinking of the seventeenth to nineteenth centuries. During the twentieth century, as explored in Chapter One, the fragmentationalist paradigm has been increasingly challenged on the grounds that its vision of reality does not match up to facts as disclosed by physicists, biologists, philosophers and others. The new paradigm, the vision of the world as a system, has gradually infiltrated such fields as health, economics, communications, environmental consciousness and, belatedly, education. The interview extracts and case studies contained in this book give some indication of new paradigm thinking operational in the school and classroom, of a shift away from transmission towards the transformation mode of teaching and learning.

It would be entirely satisfactory for the rational planner if this trend could be accounted for solely in terms of the long-term goals of particular projects or policy documents, but no such evidence exists. It is true that some educational initiatives over the last ten years have encouraged teachers to adopt global and multi-cultural perspectives and to employ more participatory and co-operative learning strategies. On the other hand, many of the more mainstream innovations – in science, maths and technology, for example – have not been exactly imbued with new paradigm thinking; in any case, on the evidence presented earlier in this chapter, one has to doubt their effectiveness as primary forces for change in schools. Our own experience as in-service educators in global education lends credence to the theory of change as an infinitely more complex, multi-dimensional process. In so many cases, some of which are cited in this book, our exposition of holistic thinking and its implications for teaching and learning has met with levels of receptivity, at a personal as well as a professional level, which go far beyond the purely cognitive appreciation of new curriculum ideas. There is a sense, shared by others working in similar fields, of tuning in to the *zeitgeist*, like plucking a violin string with exactly the right touch and tempo to give full meaning to the concerto. The process of change is neither initiated nor directed by the teacher educator: she is merely the midwife, to use a Socratic – if somewhat sexist – term, in a process of growth and creativity whose origins lie elsewhere, and whose destination is yet unknown.

> *Facilitating the change process is like sculpting a block of wood. Although we who envision the change may have images of the result we want, we do not have control; there is interplay with the wood. Our primary task as change agents is to 'raise the grain' of the material we are working with, to uncover the ideas and symbols that will contribute to the change strategy.*
>
> – Fran Peavey

During our research, many teachers reported a significant moment in their personal or professional lives when they sensed that their perspectives and assumptions had first been challenged by new paradigm vision (see Chapter Three). For some, it was through working and living abroad; for others, a personal tragedy had triggered a reassessment of values and aspirations, whilst some teachers recounted a combination of global crises and professional development as being inspirational factors. Whatever the causes, these incidents highlight the significance of the inner dimension in change. Change is not something that happens to people, it is a dynamic force in which the whole person plays a crucial role, a process in which personal values and planetary trends are interconnected and interactive.

## Towards organic change in schools

In the first two chapters we have, at various points, suggested what change in schools would be like if it was rooted in an holistic paradigm. There follows a summary of these points to serve as a checklist for educators who wish to facilitate the process of organic change.

### Organic change is multi-faceted
Change can be triggered at any level of the school system, from first year student to headteacher; once begun it will impact on the whole school, though at any stage in its development it will be subject to modulation by other members of the school community. It will spawn new change – unpredicted spin-offs which themselves will gather momentum and influence the whole school.

### Organic change makes connections

For change to have meaning for all members of the school community each must appreciate their connectedness to the whole system. Organic change involves collegiality – co-operative working and a sharing of decision-making in the classroom, staffroom, dining-hall and community centre.

### Organic change is whole person oriented

Just as the primary force for change may be intuition rather than rational planning, so the impact of change is likely to touch personal as well as professional lives. The experiences of students and teachers in other systems – the home, the community, the world – are valued as forces for change, as are their artistic, creative and spiritual dimensions. Organic change both relies upon and nurtures caring and empathy between members of the school community.

### Organic change redistributes power

Each member of the school community is potentially both agent and recipient of change. Through active involvement in the process of change, students and teachers are empowered by it. Just as individuals – from within or external to the school system – have the right to propose change, so do students and teachers have the right and the power to reject or renegotiate a change which does not have meaning for them.

### Organic change is provisional and continuous

Any proposed change is subject to further modulation as it reverberates around the school system, impacting on and being influenced by the needs and aspirations of all members. Ownership of change is therefore a collective rather than an individual matter. A change is never finally implemented; each new day, each new batch of ideas, desires and dreams ensures that change itself continuously changes.

### Organic change is self-evaluative

Through their involvement in the change process, all members of the school community are empowered to assess its effectiveness and to make any necessary adjustments. Evaluation is as much a process of self-assessment as it is an appraisal of a new policy, curriculum or teaching method.

### Organic change is natural ... and planned

Change is natural to a system, but individuals can inhibit their own or others' propensity to be part of that natural process. A combination of intuition and rational foresight is therefore required by policy and decision-makers in the school to ensure the equal participation of every member in the change process.

## AN AFFECTIONATE ALPHABET
## – SOME LETTERS FOR A SPIRIT OF OUR TIME

A *is for our Age, Aquarian, New*
B*'s barefoot economists, and Buddhist ones too*

C *is creation, our original blessing*
D*'s deep ecology, totality stressing*

E*'s experiential education, extending what's known*
F *is the feminine, coming into her own – so*

G *is the goddess, and Gaia, and greening, and*
H *is life's holiness, and holistic meaning*

I *is intermediate technology, friend of earth and*
*employment*
J *is jobs and real work, for cash and enjoyment*

K *is knowledge, knitting matter and mind*
L *is love, living Eros, renewing all kind*

M*'s meditation, the motionless movement of the mystic*
N*'s the new sciences, n-dimensional, non-mechanistic*

O*'s the order that's implicate, Omega in time*
P*'s post-positive shifting to a new paradigm*

Q *is quantum theory, Newtonian physics dissolving*
R*'s the right brain's hemisphere, reconciling, resolving*

S *is small that is beautiful, and Fritz S of great learning*
T *is Tao, transformation, and the point that is turning*

U*'s the unconscious, (Jung and Gestalt more than Freud)*
V*'s visualisation, a vehicle Jung employed*

W *is the wholeness of which all else is a part*
X *is therefore xenophilia, for the stranger an open heart*

Y *is Yin and Yang, but more Yin than Yang, and – my*
*friends – Y is you*

Z*'s the Zeitgeist I'm greeting here, but fearing for too.*
– Robin Richardson

# References

1. Department of Education and Science, *School Education in England – Problems and Initiatives* (Yellow Paper), 1976. Edited extracts in the *Times Educational Supplement*, 15 October.

2. Steadman, S. D., Parsons, C. and Salter, B. G., *A Second Interim Report to the Schools Council*, mimeo, Schools Council, 1980.

3. Jamieson, I., 'Consultancy in the Management of Curriculum Development', in Gray, H. L. (ed.), *Management Consultancy in Schools*, Cassell, 1988, 151.

4. Cooksey, G., 'Three Years with the Schools Council' in Bell, R. & Prescott, W. (eds.), *The Schools Council: A Second Look*, Ward Lock, 1975, 155.

5. Reynolds, J. & Skilbeck, M., *Culture and the Classroom*, Open Books, 1976, 107.

6. See, for example, Sarason, S., *The Culture of the School and the Problem of Change*, Allyn & Bacon, 1982.

7. Fullan, M., *The Meaning of Educational Change*, New York, Teachers College Press, 1982, 4.

8. Parsons, C., *The Curriculum Change Game*, Falmer Press, 1987, 202–212.

9. Parsons, C., *op. cit.*, 232.

10. Marris, P., *Loss and change*, New York, Anchor Press/Doubleday, 1975, 166.

11. Sarason, S., *op. cit.*, 232.

12. Fullan, M., *op. cit.*, 113.

13. Schon, D., *Beyond the Stable State*, New York, Norton, 1971, 12.

14. Lortie, D., *Schoolteacher: A sociological study*, Chicago, University of Chicago Press, 1975; findings summarised in Fullan, M., *op. cit.*, 108–9.

15. Huberman, M., Microanalysis of innovation implementation at the school level. Unpublished paper, University of Geneva, 1978, cited in Fullan, M., *op. cit.*, 27.

16. Fullan, M., *op. cit.*, 127.

17. Fullan, M., *op. cit.*, 113.

18. Elliott, J., How do teachers learn? Unpublished paper, Cambridge Institute of Education, 1979, 7, cited in Fullan, M., *op. cit.*, pp. 269–70.

19. Fullan, M., *op. cit.*, 28.

20. Miller, J., *The Holistic Curriculum*, Ontario, OISE Press, 1988, 4–6.

21. Woods, P., 'Teacher, Self and Curriculum', in *Defining the Curriculum: Histories and Ethnographies*, Goodson, I. F. & Ball, S. J. (eds.), Falmer Press, 1984, 260.

22. Seminar held at the NFER Headquarters in Slough on 11 May 1987.

23. Cited in Capra, F., *The Turning Point*, Flamingo, 1983, 20.

24. Capra, F., *op. cit.*, 20.

25. Richardson, R., 'Changing the curriculum', in Hicks, D. (ed.), *Education for Peace: Issues, Principles and Practice in the Classroom*, Routledge, 1988, 243.

My first step away from the old white man was trees. Then air. Then birds. Then other people. But one day when I was sitting quiet and feeling like a motherless child, which I was, it come to me: that feeling of being part of everything, not separate at all. I knew that if I cut a tree, my arm would bleed. And I laughed and I cried and I run all around the house. I knew just what it was. In fact, when it happen, you can't miss it. It sort of like you know what, she say, grinning and rubbing high up on my thigh.

— Alice Walker, *The Color Purple*

·CHAPTER THREE·

# Personal Change

We have argued in the first two chapters that holistic or organic change is *multi-dimensional*: to understand the process of change in schools necessitates an appreciation of its many elements and, crucially, of their interrelationships. Over the succeeding four chapters our aim is to illustrate the multi-dimensional nature of educational change through case studies of change in selected schools in England, based on interviews and research carried out by the authors as part of the Global Impact Project.[1] Many of the teachers interviewed had had some experience – through classroom teaching and in-service courses – of world studies, an educational approach which combines a global perspective in the curriculum (concern for issues to do with environment, development, human rights, peace and co-operation) with a humanistic, child-centred methodology (using participatory, affirming and co-operative techniques in the classroom). World studies, and its more holistic relation, global education, are now well established in most local education authorities in England and Wales.[2] They are leading forces in the discernible shift away from fragmentationalist forms of education.

The chapters are organised under four broad headings – personal change, institutional change, change and the local education authority, change and the external agency – which represent the 'hubs' of change: the locations of the more significant forces for change. Within chapters, and particularly towards the end of each, will be found the 'spokes': the vital connections which link various dimensions of change into one continuous and interrelated process. Thus it will be seen that change is not confined to the school or department alone, nor to the personal development of an individual teacher, though the principal focus or thrust of change may be located at any one of these levels.

It should be recognised that the model of organic change advocated in the previous chapter is an ideal which is unlikely to be found in any mainstream school at present, on account of the pervasive force of fragmentationalist thinking in education. Some all-too-familiar remnants of such thinking, from rigid subject boundaries to strictly didactic teaching, are to be found within the interview extracts cited in these chapters. There is also, however, abundant and exciting evidence of teachers and institutions breaking free from the restrictive shackles of the past by embarking upon processes of change leading towards holistic education. In this sense, the case studies cited are both representative and not representative. They provide examples of the growing number of transformatory initiatives, in schools throughout the UK, which have holism as a goal but which, as yet, are fraught with internal contradictions and inconsistencies. On the other hand, it would be misleading to suggest that these examples are commonplace in education, that the end of fragmentationalist schooling is in sight. To use the delta analogy, prominent islands of sediment are increasing in size and number, but it will be some time yet before they emerge as a new, connected land mass.

## Significant entry points

At the hub of this chapter is personal change: processes of professional transformation which have, at their focus, a questioning and re-evaluation of personal values, perspectives and beliefs. In order to move towards more holistic approaches a teacher may be faced with a fundamental reassessment of her role. Factors which contribute to such a shift may be gradual in their action but the start of the process of change can often be associated, retrospectively, with a particular event or experience – when a sudden fresh look at assumptions is made, forcing a radical rethinking of current approaches and practices. Marilyn Ferguson describes this first stage as an *entry point*: 'anything which shakes up the old understanding of the world, the old priorities. . . . The entry point experience hints that there is a brighter, richer, more meaningful dimension to life.'[3] A Newcastle primary teacher offered a powerful image for this: 'I just had to have a little chink of light before the door swung really wide open and I was flooded – I could relate it to every other aspect of my experience'.

Overseas work and travel often provide significant 'entry points'. One Dorset junior teacher remarked that her stay in India encouraged her to think of ways of teaching about

> *Believing in the possibility of real change – transformative*
> *change of our distressed world – means being willing to*
> *cultivate in our adult lives the shameless impudence of*
> *children – but a shamelessness not from innocence, and*
> *an impudence not from a mere automatic rejection of*
> *authority. Rather I mean a willingness to look with fresh*
> *eyes, to refuse to take as givens the shoulds and should*
> *nots handed down to us, and, most of all, a determination*
> *to follow through on the logical, moral consequences of*
> *what we learn.*
>
> – Frances Moore Lappé

other countries which avoided the exotic, tourist view. A secondary teacher from Cornwall reflects on a series of key moments in his personal and professional development. (See also Case Study 1).

*'When I was eighteen and about to leave school, a friend of mine said: "Come on, I'm going to go on this VSO". I said "What on earth is that?" and I managed to get myself a year's teaching in the Solomon Islands. Then when I left university, I went to work in Zambia for three years. I had to come back for family health reasons, but I was converted in Zambia to the idea that we had to educate people in environmental awareness before the good old planet was down the drain plug! So looking around for a job, I went into geography teaching – which wasn't too bad, but not exactly what I wanted to do. I started with the South-West Development Education Project, which I enjoyed; but it was only when I encountered the world studies approach in 1983 that I thought to myself: "This is what I have been looking for. This involves the human being as well as the environment; this involves a complete spectrum of growth that I need and that children need." '*

Experience of different cultural values does not, of course, necessitate leaving the British Isles. Many teachers have remarked on the profound impact of coming face to face with a set of beliefs and life experiences which are alien to their own. A Dorset middle school teacher recounts her 'entry point'.

*'I think it was coming into this school three years ago. I had never taught in a school like this. I'd been at a very middle class sort of school, and when I said I was coming here, people said: "You don't want to go there, that's awful, that's a really tough estate," and I came in a bit wary. But when I came, I felt the children were lovely kids – if you could just get them to gel, there's something there, they're*

not lost causes. I felt at one stage that I was the only stable thing in some of those children's lives, parents all remarrying and living with other people. I get the odd case of child battering, but basically the children are very warm-hearted.'

For a Bradford secondary teacher, born and bred in the city, the challenge to his own perspectives and assumptions is not new but still thought provoking.

*In its most fundamental form, of course, the politics of change is about how we actually live our own lives, and about the effect we have on the people and the microstructures of society immediately around us on whom our way of living impinges directly.*
– James Robertson

'*In our position with the sort of school and type of intake, it's not difficult to see first hand examples of inequality, social deprivation; students who are in many ways deprived and underprivileged. There is cultural diversity and clashes of culture, ideas and values. You constantly find your own ideas being challenged; things which you think are right and proper and the way you've always done it, you realise that it's not how X, Y and Z do it.*'

Clashes of cultural values in the classroom can often lead to exhibitions of prejudice and intolerance which come as a deep shock to the teacher and act as prime motivation to 'do something'.

'*I was staggered a few years ago when a Jewish colleague, teaching about the inter-war period and the rise of Fascism, ran into tremendous anti-semitism. "Wasn't Hitler rather a good thing because he had the right idea about the Jews?". She uncovered hostility about Jewish people that I found very surprising.*'
(Secondary Headteacher, North Tyneside).

'*I had a little girl in my class, lovely child, lovely family, and I was horrified one day when this beautiful, blond, blue-eyed, angel-faced child turned to another and said: "Don't play with her, she's dirty." I was so horrified to hear this angelic creature saying such a horrible thing about another lovely little girl – five year olds they were. I just felt this is something that's got to be tackled right from the beginning. That certainly motivated me to do something.*'
(Infant Teacher, Leeds)

A common element in these 'entry point' experiences is that they involve a response by the whole person, both intellectual and emotional; in fact, in so far as the entry point is motivating and energising, it can be very much a purely emotional response – the intellectual rationalisation coming later. They are experiences that seize hold of one so that a retreat into intellectual abstractions is not possible. In other words, they engage the right brain – where our perceptions, our experience of reality is integrated in context and given meaning. Thus they allow the possibility of a re-examination of the assumptions and values on which our perception of the world, our worldview, is based. It is important that those who seek to offer others experiences which may act as such 'entry points' recognise the importance of addressing the affective as well as the cognitive domain – of accessing the right as well as the left brain. In Zen teachings a tool which is often used in order to make students realise the limitations of logic and reasoning is that of paradoxical riddles called *koans*. Fritjof Capra describes the use of such a tool and compares it to Heisenberg's account of the way in which physicists in the 1920s experienced the quantum paradox.

> 'The descriptions of the koan method all emphasized that the solving of such a riddle demands a supreme effort of concentration and involvement from the student. The koan, it is said, grips the student's heart and mind and creates a true mental impasse, a state of sustained tension in which the whole world becomes an enormous mass of doubt and questioning. When I compared this description to (that of Heisenberg) I felt very strongly that the founders of quantum theory experienced exactly the same situation. . . . As in Zen, the solutions to the physicists' problems were hidden in paradoxes that could not be solved by logical reasoning but had to be understood in terms of a new awareness, the awareness of the atomic reality.'[4]

Edward de Bono's work on generative thinking also emphasises the importance of perceptions: 'The teaching of thinking is not the teaching of logic but the teaching of perception.'[5] De Bono's courses are characterised by the use of 'tools', such as metaphors, fantasy, role plays, all designed to block snap judgements and retreat into mental abstraction and generalisation, in order to help learners to 'think again', to sustain perceptual work.

## The threat of change

An 'entry point' opens up the possibility that there are other ways of looking at things; other ways of knowing. Individual 'entry points' will vary in nature and in depth: some are the resultant shock waves of a profound personal tragedy or crisis; others are fleeting moments in the classroom or in-service workshop when, through the blinding fog of normality, a new door opens and new horizons are glimpsed. Such an insight, of course, involves a relinquish-

> *I think it pisses God off if you walk by the color purple in a field somewhere and don't notice it.*
> – Alice Walker

> *I work from the premise that each of us has within us the will to make the world a better place, as well as a longing for stability. We live in a tension between these two drives. But there tend to be many more obstacles to our acting on the improvement impulse than to resting in inertia. So in my thinking I have shifted from the question 'What makes people change?' to 'What keeps people from changing'*
>
> – Fran Peavey

ment of certainty, which can feel extremely threatening – especially to those whose 'gates of change' are most heavily defended.

*'Other staff are very willing but need a lot of support with a world studies approach. It requires you to relinquish power which teachers don't like, they feel very threatened by it, they feel they will lose control – utterly wrong in my experience, but I still felt like that at first. You need to experience it to realise it's not a relinquishing of power but a shifting of power and you can easily bring the children back using the skills they have learnt.'*
(Primary Teacher, Newcastle).

*'There were very interesting comments from other teachers in the school, supply teachers and cover teachers, who said: "It's terrible, I just couldn't do it, they didn't want to listen to me, they didn't want to do anything, I couldn't get them organised, I've never seen such an undisciplined lot in my life." That was partly because of the way we were working and partly because we had children there who would actually voice an opinion, and if they felt something was not up to scratch they were quite willing to say so and the more articulate ones would actually justify it and expect you to respond.'*
(Secondary Head of Humanities, Devon)

This leap into uncertainty can be especially difficult for teachers since their traditional role rests so heavily on being expert, being an authority, having all the answers. Marilyn Ferguson notes that educational institutions are some of the least dynamic in terms of transformation, lagging behind medicine, psychology, politics and the media.[6] The threat of uncertainty may be felt particularly by people working in those disciplines, such as the sciences, which are most heavily content-dominated, where teachers' self-esteem and confidence rest on familiarity with a body of knowledge. The paradox is that we live in an age of overwhelming uncertainty and to recognise this can be profoundly liberating. 'Acknowledging our uncertainty', writes Marilyn Ferguson, 'encourages us to experiment, and we are transformed by our experiments. We are free not to know the answer, we are free to change our position, we are free not to have a position. And we learn to reframe our problems. Asking the same question again and again without success is like continuing to search for a lost object in the places we have already looked. The answer like the lost object lies somewhere else altogether.'[7] We may relinquish certainty but we gain openness, and in so doing the ability to respond to changing times.

As with anyone in an uncertain or threatening situation, teachers look for support and clarity. Some find it within the values framework of an organised religion. 'Being a committed Christian' was a not uncommon response to questions which sought to discover what were the major factors enabling teachers to tackle sensitive moral and political issues in the classroom. Anthony MacNamara describes the importance of the Christian faith for him in Case Study I.

> *Honest hope derives from a belief that positive change is possible in the world. And we will only believe this if we experience ourselves changing. The key is risk, doing that which we thought we could not do.*
>
> – Frances Moore Lappé

---

## Case Study 1

## Feeling change, changing feelings

*Anthony MacNamara, Head of English at St. Peter's School, Bournemouth, talks about the influences which have shaped his view of change.*

'I went from a traditional Catholic boys' grammar school to university where I literally let my hair down and got involved in student politics. I just had a great time getting away from all the cloying repressive aspects of my life when I was a schoolboy. To a certain extent I had that experience of joyfully breaking away. Then I settled down – got married, became a teacher!

I spent four years in Angola, three years teaching with the United Nations and one year as a shipping manager in the port of Lobito. What that did for me was to show me what it smelt like, felt like, tasted like to live amongst poverty, war, disease and demoralisation; I think the UN classified Angola as the fourth or fifth most difficult country to live in. I saw Christianity in a new light there I would say because I was so impressed by the way in which the Catholic Church supported people. But it was not the kind of conservative, pious, private Christianity that I had been nurtured in and had rejected. This was something much more exciting. It answered a lot of questions for me. I think my view of the world is very influenced by the Gospel of St. Matthew: you have to try to treat everybody, especially the weakest and most marginalised, the way you would want to treat yourself. There is a preciousness and value in everything.

And then, just like anybody else, I'm concerned by what's happening to the planet globally, to the environment; the pain caused by the injustices of racial divisions, class divisions, things like that. I have shifted from a fairly hot-headed student position of wanting change immediately to the idea of working, perhaps over a long period of time, towards change. I recognise now that there is a spiritual side to this which I would have been reluctant to admit to as an undergraduate. I find inspiration in the gospels now as much as anything else. They're the things that trigger me off; they're very real to me.

My own view of change within schools is that curriculum development imposed from the top is asking for trouble. The kind of change you need in a school is change that teachers themselves perceive as necessary and in which they have a stake – there's actually something in it for them because they've been part of it. I think staffrooms are places where, at best, curiosity about what's going on in certain areas of the school leads to a rethink, perhaps, in other areas. My understanding of how change works is that people become interested, an idea is established as having legitimacy and value; then the people who work on it, through their enthusiasm and through the fact that they've had a stake in developing it from the beginning, make it something much more real.

It doesn't happen overnight. You don't have a good multi-cultural approach to English simply by throwing out your books containing racial stereotypes. You need to change the way teachers feel about these things. Teachers should feel that they're doing something because it's right, because it's exciting and interesting, not because it's the flavour of the month.'

*Since giving this interview, Anthony MacNamara has been appointed as a Deputy Head at St. Augustine's School, Oldham.*

Other teachers were empowered through the support of and connection with colleagues, which turned a potentially threatening experience for this Devon secondary teacher into a creative force for change.

*'I came into this system and it was very new, and in some ways a bit frightening for me at first, because it was totally different. I wasn't used to kids crawling all over the classroom and actually producing something at the end of it – that was what was so startling! But the team we've got here – I know it sounds like the old proverbial pat on the back – but they are terrific and very, very supportive. They are supportive with problems and responsive to new ideas. Without the energy and enthusiasm of the 'leaders' it would have been dreadful. I would welcome carrying on teaching world studies . . . I am a convert!'*

Another Devon secondary teacher stresses the enriching aspect of opening to new ideas in a supportive environment.

'I've just rejoined the team to teach world studies and I'm enjoying it and learning a lot. It's great to be in a department where classroom practice is really very sophisticated, the didactic approach is a failure; you've got to be very lively. You get good and bad lessons, but it's challenging. I sometimes think the kids haven't understood, but they have grasped it in a way I didn't anticipate.'

> *Human solidarity is the necessary condition for the unfolding of any one individual.*
> – Eric Fromm

This teacher also highlights a crucially significant aspect of the change process: the responsiveness of students to a new idea or approach. For many teachers, particularly those whose classroom experience is one of isolation and seclusion, the quality of the students' response can powerfully inhibit or encourage further innovation. One Dorset primary teacher recounted the impact on her of trying out a co-operative activity for the first time.

'I was very impressed by one girl's reaction to the "Going Dotty" exercise. She had not talked at all in class before we did this, but this activity got through to her and she started communicating.'

Other teachers have made similar observations with regard to changes in classroom process towards more participatory, interactive learning styles. Their reflections are supported by the now considerable body of research which indicates that co-operative learning and an emphasis on creating an affirming classroom environment have considerable benefits for learning, not only in terms of personal and social development, but also academic attainment.[8]

'I'm very encouraged by the kind of interaction and level of sophistication of the interaction with students. The examples of high points are certainly higher than previous high points. It's also more obvious if kids aren't learning; before you could get very neat exercise books and no learning, now they are screaming around the classroom! I feel these methods have been more successful in conveying content as well.'
(Secondary Teacher, Devon)

'At first I thought these children are too young, they can't do things like that, and then when I tried it and found they really could I really enjoyed it. I was very apprehensive at first . . . I didn't think children of that age thought about things so deeply, I was amazed.'
(Infant Teacher, Leeds)

'Then we tried things out and could see the benefit and see the potential. These approaches helped in dealing with a

*disturbed, aggressive boy and I've started dealing with con-
flicts in the classroom in this way. I've been very encouraged
by the response.'*
(Reception Class Teacher, Leeds)

*'You go into two classrooms, one where you see a number
of fairly bored children sitting while the teacher talks and
says: "Open your book at page 43," and then you contrast
that with the situation where you go into Mr H's classroom
and they're arranged in groups, perhaps engaged in this
voyage of discovery . . . the children are so enthusiastic, they
rush in half way through break to say "Can we get set up,
we mustn't waste time," and you contrast the enthusiasm
and the interest and the real learning which takes place in
there with the rather arid, bored and monotonous "Here
we go again" of the dictatorial approach, the chalk and talk
approach. That in itself is justification.'*
(Middle School Headteacher, Leeds)

*Thumbs Up. Thumbs Down: primary
students evaluate a world studies
session.*

Justification for a participatory, co-operative learning process also comes from the consumers – students themselves.

City Engineers Photo Unit

*'The activities (on the rainforest) were quite exciting. You learn what a textbook can't tell you. Well, textbooks show pictures but they can't describe the feeling. Textbooks can't really describe what life is like.'*
(Upper Junior Student, Newcastle)

*'It's a good way, you can help other people if you're working in a group. You've got to listen to other people's opinions as well – if you've got a really strong personality, you've got to tone it down.'*
(Mark)
*'Group work helps you because in a job you have to meet lots of people and expect to work with them and accept their views – group work prepares you for that.'*
(Sharon)
*'We're allowed to say that we want and put over our own views. For example, you find out about poverty and population, put forward different views and combine them together. I find it very good. . . . I got put with one of the worst boys, and I found that if I let him do what he wanted and not tell him all the time, it was alright working together – we got on better.'*
(Michelle)
(Fifth Year World Studies Students, Devon Secondary School)

## Promoting personal change

A common strand running through these accounts of personal change, whether they be significant 'entry points' or quieter moments of self-evaluation, is that of personal involvement at all stages of the change process. In contrast to many teachers involved in curriculum development in the past, the teachers we interviewed clearly recognised that they had embarked on a learning process and were committed to it. That is not to deny that they had 'passed through the zones of uncertainty', nor that they were entirely free of doubts and misgivings. As a Devon secondary teacher put it:

*'At times I still feel that perhaps there are some children that slip through the net when we're doing this group work, that they're able to hide behind the enthusiasm and the hard work of others and put in very little in their group activity. I still get a bit taken aback when the kids are up and around the classroom, and by this frequent·noisy movement.'*

She was, nonetheless, committed to interactive learning and cited the 'support and enthusiasm' of the course innovators as the principal factor in enabling her to change her teaching style. She had been provided with an opportunity to develop the necessary skills, along with encouragement and support – all crucial factors for establishing personal meaning in educational change.

---

*I stand convicted by my own convictions.*
*We are so often scared to take and use our love.*
*I stand convicted by my own convictions.*
*You too.*
*We shrink from touching our power,*
*we shrink away,*
*we starve ourselves and each other.*
*We're scared shitless of what it could be to take and use*
*our l l love,*
*hose it on a city and world,*
*to wield and guide its spray,*
*destroying quasons, parasites, rats, viruses.*

– Adrienne Rich

---

As we have seen in this chapter, personal change for some teachers is initiated by events and influences outside their professional role, for others the entry point is provided by an 'in-service' experience. We shall explore in succeeding chapters the function of, and potential for, in-service education from the vantage point of the school, the LEA, and the external agency, but let us now consider how personal change might be stimulated by a planned course or programme. In other words, what is the role of rational planning in a process of organic change?

Many teachers have talked of the value of outside school courses, not as ends in themselves but, in the words of one Dorset secondary teacher, as 'a lever to get me thinking'. A colleague of hers, referring to the same LEA programme of residential weekends, suggested that it had 'acted as a catalyst . . . and crystalized a number of things' for him. A lever, a catalyst, a framework for clarifying ideas . . . this would seem to be the proper function of an in-service course in promoting personal change. It recognises that the change process does not begin with the course, nor does it end there; support for teachers returning to the demanding realities of the classroom is crucial. For a few, a well run in-service course oriented towards the whole person can have a powerful, even spiritual impact, as Case Study 2 illustrates. It is important to recognise again, however, that the course itself has not instigated such profound transformation, but has provided an appropriate and timely context for an individual 'entry point' to be discovered.

# Case Study 2

## A very personal experience

*Jean Pike, teacher of lower juniors at Epiphany Church of England First School, Bournemouth, talks about the impact of world studies on her personal and professional life.*

'Taking up my career again was my "entry point". I was so suppressed in my personal life, I was never allowed to realise my full potential. Then with the involvement in the world studies course and at the same time reading some of the recommended literature – such as *The Aquarian Conspiracy* – it was such an eye-opener for me. The course was really a very personal experience – it came at a time in my life when things were very difficult anyway. I found some of the experience very upsetting, there were perhaps certain things I had to resolve within my own mind. But having said that, I found those things upsetting because they made me look at my whole being, they made me evaluate things that I felt were important but that I was not able to enjoy. I can't find words to describe the experience really.

At my previous school, two staff members who had been on the world studies course ran some after school sessions. I was excited by the activities and fascinated by seeing some unusual things happening in class. I loved going around the classrooms afterwards and seeing some of the writing that came out of it; it was so powerful. I was desperate to get on this course, but couldn't as I was on a temporary contract. When I got this job at Epiphany, I persuaded the deputy head that it was essential for a new school like this to be involved in world studies. Having talked to other people who had been on the course, I certainly did expect great things from it personally. I wasn't disappointed, not at all. Really, those two weekends made you look at yourself as a person, as a wife perhaps, as a mother, whatever. It's incredible to me that some of those activities we did can actually evoke the feelings that they did.

I came back from the first weekend really so excited and almost taken over by it. But there's always the danger of leaping into school and saying, "Listen to me, I've got something to tell you all. This is wonderful – you've got to listen." I suppose I thought back to my previous school, where it was me seeing something going on and thinking, "What are they doing?", that really got me interested. Not anybody saying, "Have you heard about this?", just by actually seeing.

It was the children themselves who got other people involved. They would want to leave our area to go and talk to other teachers. They would suddenly go into a classroom and say, "I want to make you a Friendship Flower", and the teacher would say, "Well, fine, what on earth is it?", and they would drag them back. The interest came by other teachers being aware that there were things going on which seemed slightly different, slightly bizarre. The photos we've got of *Woolly Thinking* – that teacher just came with a camera and said: "What on earth's happening here? I must take some photographs!".

I've been pleased with all the activities we've actually done with the children – so much so, that I feel it's false talking about activities. It's not like that anymore, it's almost as if it's become a complete way of work. It's not what you do for world studies this week; everything that's

A display of Friendship Flowers in a Dorset middle school.

planned is planned naturally. I think you come to the realisation that if you, at an adult level, can look at yourself, can explore your own thoughts and feelings, then surely at school you can encourage children to really think and feel – about themselves, about each other and about the world. We are educating for the 21st century. We're lucky in Bournemouth, but our job is to educate children to be aware of what happens in the rest of the country and the world. Everything is connected in some way.

I've got a lot to learn from the two staff who go on the course next year. I don't want this experience to just stop.'

Another advantage of the out-of-school course is the opportunities for personal change which are provided through contact with other professionals.

*'I believed in the necessity of changing our approach, the importance of really getting to know each other and creating opportunities to hear many different points of view. But I didn't know what to do until I went on the Diploma course, I really didn't know.'*
(Infant Headteacher, Leeds)

*'I was interested in the issues but I had not come across these kinds of methods. It seemed very exciting, also meeting other teachers and being encouraged that these methods do work!'*
(Secondary Teacher, Leeds)

School-based in-service can also be a catalyst for personal change. A Dorset middle school teacher reported being 'amazed' by a Saturday staff development day on teaching and learning styles; whilst a junior teacher got 'very excited by the staff meeting on Monday night and promptly tried out some of the techniques the next day.' Someone coming into school from outside can bring in a fresh face, as well as fresh ideas.

*'It's good to have somebody new, different coming in; it makes the kids listen. You get another slant on it, it was super, it makes you look at things in a different way.'*
(Primary Teacher, Newcastle)

The success of such initiatives in promoting real change does, of course, depend upon the extent to which the immediate reactions of surprise and excitement can be converted, through practice and support, into a new and lasting teaching approach. The empowerment of an individual teacher can rarely be sustained within a department or a school which cannot both contribute to, and be enriched by, the personal change that has taken place.

# References

1. This book is the second major publication to emerge from the Global Impact Project, based at the Centre for Global Education, University of York from January 1986 to March 1989. The broad aim of the Project, funded by the World Wide Fund For Nature, was to maximise the efforts of global/holistic educators towards making the school experience more relevant to the needs and challenges faced by students in the late twentieth century. The Project's first major publication was *Earthrights: Education as if the Planet Really Mattered* (Kogan Page/WWF, 1987). The interviews from which these extracts and case studies are taken were carried out between July 1987 and April 1988.

2. More information about world studies and global education can be obtained from two handbooks for teachers: Fisher, S. & Hicks, D., *World Studies 8–13*, Oliver & Boyd, 1985; Pike, G. & Selby, D., *Global Teacher, Global Learner*, Hodder & Stoughton, 1988; or by contacting the Centre for Global Education, University of York, Heslington, York YO1 5DD, or the World Studies 8–13 Project, St. Martins College, Lancaster LA1 3JD.

3. Ferguson, M., *The Aquarian Conspiracy*, Granada, 1980, 93, 94.

4. Capra, F., *Uncommon Wisdom*, Rider, 1988, 32.

5. de Bono, E., *Learning to Think*, Penguin 1979, cited in Gough, N., 'Learning with environments . . . an ecological paradigm for education', *Green Teacher*, 8, March 1988, 14.

6. Ferguson, M., *op. cit.*, 307.

7. Ferguson, M., *op. cit.*, 114.

8. For a review of the major research, see Pike, G., & Selby, D., *op. cit.*, Ch. 2.

·CHAPTER FOUR·

# Changing Schools

## Paddling a very lone canoe. . . .

Experiences that profoundly affect the way we see the world, that challenge us and galvanise us into conducting our personal and professional lives in new ways, are a crucial element in the change process. On their own, however, they are unlikely to bring about change in schools. A long-vacation 'Third World' journey that shakes our perceptions to the core ends. What happens after 1 September? An in-service weekend course that profoundly influences the way we see teaching and learning comes to a close at Sunday lunchtime. What happens on Monday morning and in the weeks and months after that? What, in short, are the strategies necessary for sustaining personal and professional change in schools and for achieving widespread acceptance and internalisation of those changes across the whole school community?

*'There's almost a kind of danger in developing a very strong (inset course) group feeling, because when the individual isn't in that situation, when they are back in their own institution, back in their usual context, then sometimes all the normal inhibitions, the day-to-day demands of the institution can sort of blot out their ability to actually change things dramatically, and that's going to depend on the kind of framework their school, their institution, is providing them with. If they are, for whatever reason, paddling a very lone canoe, ploughing a very lone furrow, that's not easy to sustain. That's the moment an experiment really to change classroom practice can feel very difficult if there is nothing around you in the institutional context which seems to be supporting you. . . . Institutions and teachers are pretty*

*good at marginalising things which might mean they have
to work harder, change their routine, have their attitudes
challenged. Not necessarily rejecting or being totally hostile
to, but marginalising things, so that it doesn't actually affect
the ongoing rolling process of the school'.*
(Secondary Adviser)

# The Tao of Headship

Almost without exception, the teachers and advisers we
interviewed singled out the senior management team, and
particularly the headteacher, as having a key role in the
promotion or obstruction of change. Strong reservations
were expressed by one Senior Adviser for Secondary Education as to whether many headteachers had sufficient grasp
of the complex nature of change processes in schools.

*'I do worry how tenuous the growth is sometimes and I am
concerned that a lot of curriculum projects do depend on
the quality of senior management and the quality of their
thinking – their ability to think in whole school terms and
their ability to understand the whole nature of what it
means to develop the curriculum, and I have to be straight
with you on this, I think many of our headteachers and
senior management teams are sadly deficient in understanding these things, how they take these things on board, and
how they develop strategies to nurture and carry forward
that development over a period of time. They think there's a
magic solution by putting a person on a course and expecting
miracles the day after. . . . They're totally unaware of the
processes which have to be gone through before you actually
do begin to change attitudes and ingrained habits of teaching, classroom organisation and all the rest.'*

A teacher who had experienced the introduction of world
studies at two Dorset middle schools compared its successful development at her new school where the headteacher
was consistantly supportive, with the faltering progress at
her previous school where the head had offered lip-service
but little else. 'The support from the head was not total.
It didn't need his support at the beginning, but it seems to
be dying now because he's not fully behind it.' A Newcastle
junior teacher recalled the cynicism she and her colleagues
had to contend with when the headteacher, ostensibly
behind the introduction of world studies, failed to attend
a staff meeting at which the philosophy and practice of
world studies was to be introduced to the whole staff.

The headteacher's change agency role was generally viewed
as one of legitimizing the change process, of providing a

---

*The wise leader knows better than to be neurotic and self-centred. Potency comes from knowing what is happening and acting accordingly. Paradoxically, freedom comes from obedience to the natural order.*

*Since all creation is a whole, separateness is an illusion. Like it or not, we are team players. Power comes through co-operation, independence through service, and a greater self through selflessness.*

– John Heider, *The Tao of Leadership*

---

context of security and challenge within which change could flourish, of providing moral support for other change agents within the school and of sustaining the momentum of change in both the short and long term.

'The single most significant factor without a question of a doubt is that we have in our principal somebody who supports what we're doing. It really is true – he's just made it quite clear from the start that he backs what we're doing, he supports us, so we've done our work in a climate where we feel our work is valued and appreciated and that is enormously important.'
(Secondary Head of Department, Dorset)

'Staff here are informed, politically aware in the widest sense; they look ahead and try and anticipate, and part of my role is to encourage them to do that – not to get involved in day to day routines but to look ahead and say: "This is the way the world is moving, what are we doing about it in the interest of our youngsters?" '
(Secondary Headteacher, North Tyneside)

'I came in January 1982 and took an initiative by bringing together people from geography, history and business studies and said to them that whenever, wherever we look at the world there are certain question marks. Why do people live or act the way they do? Whenever people have lived together they have had to face certain problems – that has not and will not change. That was the basis . . . I haven't moved the school; I've sown some seeds, and they fell in fertile ground.'
(Secondary Headteacher, Devon, on his part in the development of a World Studies GCSE course)

Attendance of senior management on an out-of-school inset course was put forward by a number of teachers and advisers as an important way of signalling to staff that the envisaged change really mattered. In one Dorset middle

*What we call leadership consists mainly of knowing how to follow. The wise leader stays in the background and facilitates other people's process. The greatest things the leader does go largely unnoticed. Because the leader does not push or shape or manipulate, there is no resentment or resistance.*
– John Heider, *The Tao of Leadership*

school, both the headteacher and his deputy attended a year-long 'occasional day' multi-cultural education course. The effects on the school were dramatic as an enthusiastic and influential alliance was forged between senior management and two teachers attending a parallel world studies course. Within the academic year world studies had gained widespread acceptance in the school, an equality of opportunity document was in preparation and there had been staff agreement to jettison hundreds of library books held to be racist. After attending a two-year part-time Diploma course on global and multi-cultural education, one infant headteacher in Leeds proceeded to take her colleagues with her in virtually transforming the school from top to bottom (see Case Study 3, p. 78).

Headteachers who have been prepared to experiment with organic forms of organisation (see page 29) appear to have been most successful in achieving thoroughgoing curricular and methodological reform. Implicit and explicit in their approach has been an insistence on devolved and shared ownership of the change process; an acceptance that change itself is a learning process in which risks will have to be taken and mistakes inevitably made; a readiness to create an affirmative and supportive climate so that people are prepared to take risks and a recognition that change is a gradual affair in which, first, new materials, practices and behaviours and, subsequently, new beliefs and understandings will be embraced.

Several headteachers emphasised the importance of creating a supportive and democratic climate within which change could take place. Just as students needed to be affirmed and empowered if they were to realise their full potential, so did teachers.

*'Why aren't there any butterflies in this field? Answer: we haven't got the right plants because of, for example, pesticides. The solution is to go back to original conditions, then once the plants are there, the butterflies will appear. The other route is to catch butterflies and put them there, but then they die. Teachers can do the right thing, if they are working in the right conditions. Two things: 1. They need to feel their ideas are acted on; that they call the tune in terms of innovation and their opinions are important. 2. They need support when they go out on an educational limb.'*
(Secondary Headteacher, Bradford)

*'I've got to be with staff the way I would want them to work with children. If I am affirming them they will realise*

*how good it feels to be affirmed.'*
(Primary Headteacher, Newcastle)

'*We have a community of teachers who believe in the importance of what they do. They believe their job is significant – bringing life to young people. We have generated that sense of belief in the importance and significance of what we do – that in itself has helped enormously.'*
(Secondary Headteacher, North Tyneside)

'*Confidence of staff is the most important thing. If they are doing what they enjoy and then see the students enjoying it, it's all good positive strokes. I try to get across the fun and joy of learning. . . . Change is not threatening once you've got your staff enjoying coming to work. But I do think that you can't do anything unless you put a lot of emphasis on your communication skills and your support for staff. So really it becomes much easier now, because instead of having to get it all going you just have to keep the morale high, which you can do by motivating staff. But it's so easy now because people are basically doing what they want to do. By involving everybody, when change comes about, it is* their *change.'*
(Secondary Headteacher, Devon)

A Dorset secondary headteacher saw his role in the change process as that of first encouraging and then networking a range of initiatives in the school. Staff that became involved in the different initiatives – groups of 'conspirators', islands in the delta – had to be connected, thus creating a critical mass for change.

'*The informal approach is very useful in raising awareness. But I don't think that's good enough, and I don't think that just simply organising a series of different meetings is good enough either. At the moment, there is a tendency to dislike yet another meeting about this and yet another meeting about that, so I think just organising meetings is not a very subtle approach. I would prefer to see us actually picking up specific initiatives which begin to involve different members of staff, drawing these together to form a coherent picture and then using that as the basis for writing a coherent policy!'*

*Main text continued on page 80*

# Case Study 3

## Great oak trees can start in the nursery!

*Sheila Simmons, Headteacher at Ninelands Lane Infants School, Garforth, Leeds, describes the effect her involvement in global education has had upon her school. The case study is compiled from interview material and extracts from her Diploma report,* The Development of Global and Multi-cultural Education in Ninelands Lane Infant School, *University of York, 1987.*

'Ninelands Lane Infant School has a roll of 150 children of which less than one per cent are black. Staff concern to reflect the multi-cultural nature of British society in their work has for some time been deeply felt but, until recently, there was a feeling of powerlessness, inadequacy and ignorance about dealing with these matters.

In Summer Term 1985 I attended a six-week course for headteachers at the Yorkshire and Humberside Regional Headship Unit (RHU) at Woolley Hall, near Wakefield, and had the opportunity to make a special study of multi-cultural education in primary schools. I returned to school but once again I could only express concern and share with staff the feelings I had that something must be included in the curriculum to help our children be free of racial intolerance and have positive attitudes to other people of whatever creed, colour or culture. I had a desire to do something constructive but I was unable to envisage what could be done. With hindsight I see that this period in limbo was helpful in my relationship with staff.

In September 1985 I began a two-year part-time 'outreach' Diploma course in Global and Multi-cultural Education facilitated by staff from the Centre for Global Education at the University of York. Centre staff had contributed a two-day input to the RHU course and my experience then had encouraged me to apply to join the Diploma group. From September to December the Diploma course seemed to have no relevance to infant practice. I spent Tuesday evenings being introduced to experiential learning, simulation games, role play and co-operative learning. Whilst I found the theory very interesting and some of the games fun, I also felt disturbed, uncomfortable, reluctant and pressured in many of the practical learning situations in which we engaged. When, three days before my return from holiday in January 1986, I thought of two practical ideas for use with infants, I was overjoyed. Had I at last opened a door? Would these ideas fit comfortably into the school's curriculum, methodology and ethos?

The teaching staff agreed to embark on an holistic approach to develop and broaden the child's concept of self and the world we live in and to involve the parents wherever possible. During Spring and Summer Term 1986, books of classroom practice in multi-cultural education, equal opportunities, development education and conflict resolution were purchased for the staff bookshelf. They were studied and discussed and provided a starting point for experimental work in the classroom. Critical appraisal of the current curriculum was undertaken and, despite awareness of personal shortcomings, there was much taking place in school of a global nature that needed to be acknowledged, evaluated and developed. Each teacher agreed to keep a record book of any work undertaken that could be described as 'multi-cultural' or 'global' and also a Child Study Book monitoring one child's response to ongoing classroom work. By the end of Spring Term 1986, staff were enthusiastic about their new work. They personally felt a new awareness and recognised that the global/multi-cultural work undertaken should be developed and become an integral part of the curriculum, preferably with the parents' knowledge and approval.

At the parent/staff meeting held in the Spring Term the opportunity was taken to raise the awareness of parents to the global needs of their children. After telling parents that teaching staff had come to believe that if children were happy with themselves, they were more likely have positive attitudes to others, regardless of race, creed, colour, age or sex, the parents were asked to form discussion groups. Many honest and important points flowed from each group. This initial parent/staff sharing of concerns gave the teaching staff assurance that their new work would be welcomed.

Colleagues agreed that Autumn 1986 was to be our designated time for introducing children to a broader perspective wherever we saw the opportunity. There was to be no scheme, timetable or set approach. We would use and add to the activities and methods already trialled.

Experiences would continue to be shared on a regular basis and the whole school initiative in global infant education would be carefully monitored. There was general agreement that the heart of the new work would be 'Circle Time' – sharing circles to develop listening and speaking skills, to build group trust and to pool feelings, experiences, ideas and information. 'Circle Time' is now a regular component of each class in the school. Circles are used to affirm the qualities and abilities of each class member ('I'm happy to be me because. . . .'); to develop mutual awareness through the expression of feelings ('I feel sad when . . .'); to brainstorm (e.g. everybody contributing some impression of the sunflowers the class had grown prior to work on a class poem). They are also used to resolve class conflicts. One day I arrived in class to find the dinner lady with a pair of plimsolls she had retrieved from the toilet. Stephen admitted he was the culprit. I decided to use the circle to see if the class could resolve the situation. Four questions were put in turn to the circle – 'what do you think about Stephen putting Claire's pumps in the toilet?'; 'how would you feel if they were your pumps?'; 'why do you think he did it?'; 'what do you think should be done about it?'. When Stephen's mother came to school, the circle record was a great help to me. I told her how the other children felt about it. We were able to discuss the matter thoroughly and she was given the copy of the circle discussion that Stephen had copied down.

In Autumn 1986 staff and parents came together to experience a range of activities themselves. In all, there were twelve meetings and each parent received an invitation to attend at least two. All meetings were well attended with 86 out of a possible 123 families represented over the whole series. How have the meetings affected parents? I have observed at ordinary parent/staff meetings since that parents and teachers are noticeably friendlier and that the meetings are much more a co-operative effort. Parents contribute; staff contribute; we all listen to each other and everyone is responsible for the progress of the meeting. An effective global education change strategy must, in my view, involve the parents.

Since 1982 Ninelands Lane has also had a nursery school. Nursery and infant school are the second and third steps in the children's global education. In providing an environment in which children can learn to value themselves and others we are turning them towards world citizenship as well as encouraging them to become good members of their immediate community. Great oak trees can start in the nursery! The first step, however, starts with the family. The family's influence also remains with a child long after nursery and infant education has passed. That is why parents must be informed and included in the global and multi-cultural education of their children if it is to be effective.

School teaching staff could not have put the global approach into practice without the staff meetings devoted to passing on what I had absorbed from the regular Diploma course workshops. It is incumbent on local education authorities who wish to address areas such as anti-racist and multi-cultural education to provide in-service experience for teachers. Without inset help, maybe most teachers would feel as we did at Ninelands before 1985 – inadequate and afraid we might add to prejudice. Most teachers have good intentions but this is a poor substitute for positive professional help.'

*Sheila Simmons has since been appointed Headteacher of the combined Ninelands Lane Infant and Junior School.*

# The Ripple Principle

Change, a number of teachers and headteachers were at pains to point out, is best effected through a judicious combination of formal and informal approaches. A startling example of this 'two-pronged' approach was offered by staff at a Dorset middle school. Two teachers returning enthused from a long weekend LEA world studies course – their first contact with a year-long programme – initially encountered a solid wall of indifference, if not hostility, from colleagues. 'My first day visit,' explained the recently-appointed deputy headteacher, 'was on the day after they'd been for the first weekend. They came into the staffroom and they were quite bubbly about what they'd done and they were put down straight away by at least five staff, and I thought "Goodness!".' Shortly afterwards they met with their (very supportive) headteacher and identified a range of informal strategies aimed at firing staff interest in world studies.

It was agreed that a whole-morning session involving inter-active learning approaches would be held each week in the hall, a thoroughfare which other teachers had to use to reach the staffroom. The sessions were to involve the classes taught by the two teachers (a range of 8–10 year olds). It was also agreed that work arising out of the sessions would be prominently displayed in the hall. The learning activities used – a blend of self-esteem and co-operative group activities – soon began to attract interest. 'The teachers came through the hall and some got a bit involved, stopped and asked what was going on.' As the displays built up in the

S. Siger

*Part of the world studies display in the school hall.*

S. Siger

*Students engage in co-operative group machines in the school hall.*

hall – displays on feelings, conflict in school and gender issues – colleagues paid increasing attention. An assembly on jumping to conclusions, based on the world studies work, fed into the process and before long other staff were asking if they could attend the world studies lessons.

*'Having lots of displays in the hall has provoked a lot of comment. There's maybe one member of staff who hasn't commented, but even he came to me this morning and said could he observe one of my lessons where I was putting active learning into practice. I said, "Yes, of course, come on in."'*

The school, set in an area of social deprivation, has a student population, on the whole, lacking in self-esteem and positive personal relationships. Many students are intolerant and conflictual in approach. 'The children are not well motivated towards each other, for all sorts of reasons, perhaps reasons of family background where they may well have to fight their corner to get anything, or they're in a house where there is a great deal of tension of even physical violence and they grow up in a very selfish way.' What perhaps fired interest in world studies more than anything else was the noticeable change in attitudes and behaviours amongst most of the students involved in the world studies lessons. One teacher remarked upon the ability of the children to work well together. They were 'beginning to think of other people's needs'. They were 'thinking kind thoughts'. The headteacher was quite categorical that 'the first-year class that does world studies is a far better unit than the other two first-year classes' and another teacher wondered how the (very difficult) fourth year 'would have turned out if they had had a world studies programme earlier'. Colleagues began to invite the two world studies teachers to conduct lessons with their classes.

Interest having grown sufficiently, the process was taken a stage further when it was agreed that two staff training days would be devoted to world studies and teaching and learning styles. The days were to be led by the two world studies teachers. For those who had already become receptive to world studies through the informal change strategies employed, the days were extremely significant and helped consolidate their interest. 'Those with open minds got a lot out of it, but the few against change were resistant. "I don't intend to change the way I teach. I teach the way I teach. If they don't learn it's their fault".' The two teachers, who had declared themselves 'petrified' before the first training day, employed interactive group approaches broken by short inputs. It was important that 'message' and 'medium' were in harmony.

'It was quite obvious that some people didn't want to play, but the world studies techniques that they developed overcame that. They didn't become confrontational. They didn't allow themselves to be rattled and gradually things changed. I wouldn't say it shifted them but it's given them lots to think about. That's the ripple principle.'

On one of the inset days, lesson plans for the whole-morning sessions were distributed. Some staff subsequently tried the activities out in their own classrooms. Another important outcome was the decision to restructure the fourth-year humanities course so that it encompassed a greater diversity of teaching and learning styles.

'My feeling about it is that as with lots of these things, if I had said it would be introduced throughout the school, it may well have been introduced, but I don't think it would have been effective, whereas the way we've done it – it's caused ripples and other people in the school are taking ideas and are beginning to think in a more active way in the classroom, so that the activities in the school are changing.' (Headteacher)

---

*Why is the sea king of a hundred streams?*
*Because it lies below them.*
*Therefore it is the king of a hundred streams.*

*If the sage would guide the people, he must serve with humility.*
*If he would lead them, he must follow behind.*
*In this way when the sage rules, the people will not feel oppressed;*
*When he stands before them, they will not be harmed.*
*The whole world will support him and will not tire of him.*

*Because he does not compete,*
*He does not meet competition.*

– Lao Tsu

---

The senior management team were at one in thinking that further pairs of staff should be invited to go on the LEA world studies course in subsequent years so as to build up sufficient commitment and expertise to achieve a 'critical mass' for change. They were clear that hard work would lie ahead in 'formalising' the world studies approach across the school. In this process, a 'statement of values would be important' as would liaison with parents and the identification of aims, objectives and a range of activities suitable for different year groups. Team teaching was suggested as perhaps the best means of involving a dwindling rump of traditional staff threatened by the spread of world studies topics and activities.

In a first school a similar path towards change was followed by two teachers returning from the same world studies course. Backed by a very supportive headteacher and 'aware of the danger of leaping into school saying "Listen to me, I've got something to tell you all",' the two teachers sought to interest colleagues through ongoing informal contact in the staffroom, through displays of students' work and through planning their team-led world studies sessions in the staffroom in the hearing of other staff. There is clear evidence that such strategies stirred interest, but of critical importance in the change process in this school were the students themselves. Their infectious enthusiasm for world studies approaches influenced other staff who also came to realise that they had been operating from a far too limited conception of their children's potential.

*'I think what has been highlighted more than anything else for me is that we often underestimate the potential of younger children. It's all too easy to give them the mundane, trite, mediocre, wishy-washy work we give them sometimes, which is actually way below what they can actually achieve. I think this is where world studies can help; where the resources will help the children to develop lively enquiring minds, which they're capable of doing, and which I certainly must admit, and I'm sure other colleagues would, we often underestimate.'*
(Headteacher)

*'They (the students) would want to leave our area and go and talk to some of the other teachers about it. They would suddenly go into a classroom and say "I want to make you a Friendship Flower" and the teacher would say "Well, fine, what on earth is it?" and they'd actually bring them back and say "Look!". Without me suggesting anything, the children had wanted to go and ask the teachers to come and join in and I think the interest came from there. The interest came by actually being aware that there were things going on which seemed slightly different, slightly bizarre.... From there other teachers questioned us, asked to borrow world studies books and asked for staff meetings to share activities.'*

*'I wish I had more opportunity to see what they have been doing, because the results really show a very clear difference in the work and motivation of their children to others – they are more co-operative. It is a very exciting way of working and has benefits right across the curriculum.'*
(Infant Teacher)

*'One of the benefits of an open-plan school is that whatever goes on can be seen by other teachers, children and parents. What they have been doing is more noticeable in this environment. The recent staff meeting was one of the most useful things; it should have happened earlier. The two-pronged approach has whetted appetites – the formal in-service and the informal interest in what is going on in the school.'*
(Deputy Headteacher)

In one Newcastle junior school, a teacher appointed with special responsibility for promoting world studies, saw her role as one of sensitively and gradually helping colleagues to accommodate to change. 'I didn't rush in in the first four weeks and blather about it. I went softly, softly. I took my time in a natural sort of way.' An important early step she saw to be that of identifying and establishing a good working rapport with a sympathetic staff member. 'I had singled out one member of staff whom I knew would be a very positive support for whatever I was going to do. She came on a (world studies) weekend and we started working on a joint plan.' A partnership was thus established that not only began to try out ideas in the classroom but also to share ideas and experiences with colleagues in a very informal, downbeat way, often over a cup of coffee in the staffroom. 'It was a case of gradually creating awareness of what the methodology and the issues were.' Another important strategy was to build upon colleagues' interest by letting them see relevant resources. 'I'm feeding in things – one of them is very interested in environmental issues and animal care and I've let her see *Green Teacher* magazines and things like that.' A further step was to encourage colleagues to fit particular activities into ongoing project work. This at first involved going into their classrooms and facilitating the activities personally, but as teachers acquired confidence in handling co-operative, interactive learning approaches, it became sufficient to supply them with good ideas and resources. 'Teacher handbooks and packs – one colleague's using *Yanomamo* and the *Rainforest Pack* – for a teacher who's had a little bit of a taster and wants to go on, they give an awful lot of back-up support.' Woven into the change strategy had been two after-school in-service workshops on world studies for the whole staff, the first led by the teacher with responsibility herself, the second by an in-service trainer from an external agency. 'The staff responded very well. The format was interactive and far more useful than to be presented with very little time for discussion.' At the time we visited the school, plans were being laid to link the separate world studies and multi-cultural education developments in the school through two staff training days. The 'conspirators' were recognising their connections.

The teacher with responsibility for world studies had worked alongside other teachers during her non-contact time. No other time had been set aside for her to perform the floating in-service training she was convinced could be a major force for change.

*'I think it would be much better if people with responsibilities for curriculum development got time to be released and to go into other classes as a fairly regular thing. It raises the whole status. That's one of the biggest drawbacks, trying to implement change, and finding the time to support teachers in the classroom, co-plan and then actually conduct the activity with them. I think it's crucial to have that extra time, but it really doesn't seem to be possible.'*

The teacher's feelings accord with research findings suggesting that 'providing teachers with more "non-contact" time can be an effective way of helping teachers to introduce and sustain curriculum change'.[1] Non-contact time for teachers earmarked as key change agents was a feature noticeable by its absence in the schools we visited.

The teacher also felt that her role as change agent would have been in some ways easier had she been given a role specification 'to which everybody could have recourse'. There had been occasional tense moments with some colleagues, in part caused by the confusion surrounding her wide-ranging responsibility. On the other hand, she recognised the dangers inherent in a 'too clearly defined role in that it might deny access to areas of importance'.

An approach to change sometimes employed at secondary level is what we might describe as the 'engine room' strategy. This involves the promotion of change within one department as a first phase of change with that one department playing a pivotal role in the next, whole school, phase. One Dorset secondary Head of Department argued strongly – and successfully – in favour of a group of his staff attending an LEA world studies course.

*'I made the case rightly or wrongly that there was a danger that the experience would be diluted, that if individuals went from individual departments, it would not be the same as four or five people, all of whom talk a great deal and exchange ideas, going together and seeing what happens within that department, and I have no doubt that the enormous interest that generated amongst ourselves has paid off. It has not been diluted.'*

In retrospect, he was to accept that he had 'coveted' the world studies course in terms of the benefits for his department rather than thinking holistically of the school's needs. A curriculum development project had, accordingly been devised for the following year to be based in the department but with the intention of drawing in other curriculum areas. A Devon secondary school was using its social studies department's interdisciplinary World Studies GCSE course as the 'engine room' in the development of a 75% entitlement core curriculum aimed at developing 'autonomous individuals in an interdependent world'. The headteacher was doubtful whether the cross-curricular impact had, in fact, matched expectations. There seem to be particular problems attached to introducing a global perspective across the curriculum once a particular department has established a well-run interdisciplinary course focussing on global themes. One Leeds middle school we visited had developed an exciting and popular environmental studies course running over four years. Classroom work regularly involves group and simulation activities. Attached to the course is a woodland environmental area and wildlife garden set in the school grounds. The senior management team's hope was that the themes and teaching styles in environmental studies would permeate other areas of the curriculum. This had not happened. There was some resistance arising out of teachers' lack of confidence in handling interactive teaching/learning activities and unfamiliar topics, but there was also a feeling 'in some staff that these issues are dealt with in environmental studies, so there is no need for them to get involved.' (Headteacher). As the name suggests, the 'engine room' strategy is perhaps too mechanistic an approach to achieve the depth of change required for 'whole person, whole planet' education.

As we have seen, the change process can be expedited by providing opportunities for staff to come together as a group to look afresh at the way the school operates. Especially valuable in this respect are away-from-school residential weekends as they allow for the informal contact

*Main text continues on page 90*

Simon Warner

Simon Warner

## Afterwards

When the Present has latched its postern behind my tremulous stay,
And the May month flaps its glad green leaves like wings,
Delicate-filmed as new-spun silk, will the neighbours say,
'He was a man who used to notice such things'?

If it be in the dusk when, like an eyelid's soundless blink,
The dewfall-hawk comes crossing the shades to a light
Upon the wind-warped upland thorn, a gazer may think,
'To him this must have been a familiar sight.'

If I pass some nocturnal blackness, mothy and warm,
When the hedgehog travels furtively over the lawn,
One may say, 'He strove that such innocent creatures should come to no harm,
But he could do little for them; and now he is gone.'

Åke Lindau, Ardea, London

Simon Warner

If, when hearing that I have been stilled at last, they stand at the door,
Watching the full-starred heavens that winter sees,
Will this thought rise on those who will meet my face no more,
'He was one who had an eye for such mysteries'?

And will any say when my bell of quittance is heard in the gloom
And a crossing breeze cuts a pause in its outrollings,
Till they rise again, as they were a new bell's boom,
'He hears it not now, but used to notice such things'?

– Thomas Hardy

which enables staff to get to know one another better. Such experiences are important in the creation of a more trusting and, hence, more secure climate: a climate in which staff are more likely to feel able to take a few risks and step outside the tried and tested ways with which they are familiar. They are important, too, in the development of a shared and owned philosophy.

*'The next training session is going to be two residential days – residential so that staff have time to get to know each other more informally.'*
(Primary Headteacher, Newcastle)

*'The whole staff is to be immersed for a weekend – it's important to experience world studies fully for yourself.'*
(Middle School Teacher, Dorset)

*'We're certainly not a democratic school; I wouldn't claim that but we talk a lot. Our original aims and objectives were worked out collectively, we went away for a weekend as a staff and talked about what we believed the needs of the children were in relation to the world in which they live now and as it's likely to be. 85–90% of the staff came on the weekend. We've had two weekends in the last six years where we've talked about what we ought to be providing in terms of a learning environment.'*
(Secondary Headteacher, North Tyneside)

One school we visited had gone out of its way to provide the right ambience for out-of-school inset work.

*'We're trying to build an inset programme. I've booked several sessions at a local hotel. Groups can go down after school (3.30), have tea and cakes, followed by the meeting, followed by dinner and wine (7.30–8.00). It has worked very well. You get an extended session in new surroundings which couldn't work in school.'*
(Secondary Inset Co-ordinator, Devon)

The advent of the staff training – or 'Baker' – day provides a regular opportunity for in-service work involving a whole staff; an opportunity rarely or never grasped in very many schools in the past. Where these days are well used and designed to meet the perceived and expressed needs of the teachers themselves – rather than being something that the LEA or school hierarchy imposes without consultation – they can provide a powerful 'entry point' for change.

*'We've had days on anti-racist education, multi-cultural, equal opportunities and so on. These tended to be issues*

*which we as a staff felt we should be addressing, so the initiative has come from the school rather than from the LEA, which I prefer anyway because, if it does, you are addressing perceived needs, rather than reacting to imposed needs. Very often these days have involved contributions from staff within the school, so there is a fair amount of sharing of ideas. We have also had outside advisers giving an input. Very much I would see the future of the in-service training day, Baker day, as meeting needs perceived, identified by the school, addressed by the school and then seeking other resources, human etc., and calling on groups who can offer some kind of expertise.'*
(Secondary Headteacher, North Tyneside)

There was general agreement that in-service days on global education and related fields were far more effective if they emerged as the natural outcome or extension of the kind of informal, grassroots development described earlier. It was also felt that there were real dangers if the process stopped with the one-off in-service day. A powerful in-service experience needed reinforcement, not only through further inset, but also through action at a variety of levels within the school. To create enthusiasm and raise expectations amongst a wider group of staff and not to follow through could breed disaffection towards the initiative and could possibly de-skill those teachers who needed somewhere to turn when things failed to quite work out in class as they had promised to on the in-service day.

Staff attendance on residential courses organised by the local education authority or an external agency was widely held to be a potentially powerful contribution to the change process, as long as the teachers were given senior and middle management support on their return. Most teachers felt it was far less daunting and far more productive if two or more staff members attended the same course. 'You get more than twice the value if *two* teachers go on the same course.'

*Main text continues on page 96*

# Case Study 4

## Co-operating for a Change!

*This case study has been written by Alan Simpson, Deputy Headteacher of West Walker Primary School, Newcastle.*

West Walker Primary School lies in a designated 'Social Priority Area' in the east end of Newcastle upon Tyne. The area has a 35% unemployment rate, low morale and much evidence of disadvantage. The road which runs past the school gates once led to a thriving shipyard – now dismantled. In the past, vandalism in the school was high, broken windows commonplace. The community around the school, in common with the children, suffered from low self-esteem and little concept of co-operation. Friction between children was a regular occurrence.

Norma Redfearn was appointed Head Teacher of West Walker in January 1986. Coming as she did from a nearby school, she knew the area well and was determined to introduce many new initiatives in an effort to establish a school geared to serving not only the children but the community as a whole. Her aims, reached in discussion with staff, were as follows:

☐ to create a stimulating, interesting environment which would aid learning;

☐ to change the attitudes of children, parents, teachers and the community towards the school;

☐ to put the building to uses which would best serve the community;

☐ to help the members of the community to fulfil their potential and offer them an outlet for developing their skills;

☐ to encourage the community to play an active role in decision-making.

At the outset, two factors helped us facilitate change. The Newcastle Arts and Recreation Department were developing the bank of the Tyne between the school and the river into a Riverside Park. Secondly, there was under-utilised space within the school building on account of falling rolls.

One of the first priorities was to create school grounds which were attractive and educationally stimulating. It was realised that if any scheme was to be successful then the children, parents and members of the wider community had to be actively involved.

In Autumn 1986, Newcastle Architecture Workshop, a charitable organisation, was contacted to assist in improving the school grounds. The Workshop introduced us to a group of students from Newcastle University School of Architecture who undertook studies in the school and developed initial ideas for making the school and its surroundings more attractive and useful to the local community. Their suggestions were enthusiastically welcomed by the school governors and the Walker Priority Area team who requested the Workshop to undertake further consultations and to develop plans and costings.

Since January 1987, Workshop teachers and a landscape architect have worked with pupils, parents and teachers in developing a scheme for the school grounds. Work was carried out, involving the top junior class, in soil analysis and plant growing techniques.

Later a project was developed to investigate play needs in the area and play value. This involved consulting all the children in the school. The educational value of the whole scheme was adopted as a case study by the national research project 'Learning through Landscapes' which had the support of the D. E. S. and the Countryside Commission.

Whilst work was being undertaken with the children, discussions were held with parents to elicit their wishes as regards landscaping, play-provision on the site and community needs.

A workshop was held which involved governors, parents, teaching staff, the Workshop, the Walker Priority Team and other interested agencies. As a result, the school and its grounds emerged as the key to community interest and future use of the Walker Riverside Park. Lying as it does alongside the major new access to the Park, the school would serve as a centre for educational use, with a warden based at the Field Studies Centre now being developed within the school building.

Following consultations, the Workshop submitted an outline landscaping scheme and costing to the Walker Priority Area team. Funding was approved and later sanctioned by the Department of the Environment for landscaping and community seating facilities as the first phase of the development of the site.

It was then possible to achieve the first element of the landscaping scheme, which consisted of a landscaped mound to create shelter, enclosure and variety of shape on the exposed western side of the school. This took place in May 1987 and gave encouragement to the school and community as they saw their plans beginning to take shape.

It was then agreed that the work of carrying out further consultations and producing detailed designs and costings for implementation should continue through Newcastle Architecture Workshop. In response, the Workshop produced a programme leading to implementation.

The fourth-year teacher, Hilary Tucknott, already deeply involved in the work with her class, wrote to numerous charitable organisations to raise funds to buy trees and shrubs with often positive results. At the same time, the children themselves grew plants from seeds and raised more money from sales of work. These efforts culminated in the children, parents and governors planting some 400 suitable shrubs and trees around the school grounds to a plan drawn up by the Workshop.

A pond was excavated and a wild life garden created in a corner of the grounds, whilst nearby a picnic area was established with tables and seating.

The next phase in the development of the school grounds will be the creation of a play area. Parents and children have been involved in surveying local needs and developing a brief for the play facilities. The children working in conjunction with the Workshop drew up plans/models of what they thought the play area should be like. Their ideas were incorporated into plans by the Workshop for the play area. There will be two linked play areas providing a varied and stimulating range of equipment with safety surfacing. It is envisaged that these areas will be heavily used, both during and outside school time.

*Top junior students working in the environmental garden.*

City Engineers Photo Unit

Simultaneously with the development of the grounds, work began on alterations to the wing of the school to be used by the community. These alterations were funded by Employment Initiatives and the work carried out by Community Programmes.

Three teaching areas were developed into a snack bar, an adult learning/leisure centre and a field study centre. Toilets were altered to allow access for the handicapped. A disused staffroom was wired as a computer centre, while an area was partitioned off and furnished with shelves and cupboards to serve as a library/reading room. Parents are already using the wing for dressmaking, needlework, pyrography and meetings. We were fortunate in acquiring a mobile classroom and this has been furnished and equipped as a creche.

*Top infants working on a co-operative shapes activity based on an idea from the Centre for Global Education.*

City Engineers Photo Unit

It was fortuitous that at the time we were developing the grounds and building, the Walker area schools became involved with the Centre for Global Education at York University (see Case Study 7).

The work on global education has continued and now forms the basic ethos of the school. Centre staff continue to act as consultants to the school. They have readily given advice on how the development of West Walker School site can be utilised for global education purposes. Their suggestions include:

☐ recording the process of development;

☐ relating what is happening at West Walker to global environmental issues – pollution of the environment has had a severe effect on Walker;

☐ power and decision-making – who decides what in the family, classroom, school and community?

☐ gender issues – who is doing what in the development work?

☐ evaluating how people's use of the various areas changes.

What point have we reached?

The major landscaping has taken place; the wing of the school has been altered; groups of parents are actively involved in various schemes. But of prime importance is the *change in attitude*. Children are beginning to develop some esteem for their own and other's efforts. Although quarrels still exist, they are far less frequent. The *positive* attitude has spread to the parents who now feel a sense of 'belonging'. They have grown in confidence, having met with HMIs, advisors and city inspectors, and are eager to put forward their views and ideas as they feel they are now valued. A parent governor recently accompanied the headteacher to a conference to meet Kenneth Baker. The parents are taking the initiative in raising funds for the school. A parent willingly gives up his time in coaching the football club.

The community at large is also sitting up and taking notice. One pensioner who is the neighbour-hood watch contact has taken the school under his wing and keeps an eye on it in the absence of a resident caretaker. The same good neighbour is a keen naturalist and shares his knowledge and enthusiasm with the children. The school is involved with the community sharing its art with the local church and even having an artist working with a class. Their efforts have been displayed in one of the city museums. During the past three years much progress has been made, both physical and attitudinal. However, there is still a long way to go.

The aim is to see every room actively utilised, greater involvement of parents, both mums and dads, further development and fulfilment of the potential of members of the community; also to create a stimulating environment for the children to learn in and to promote the participation of all in their education. Above all – a growth in positive attitudes on the part of all concerned. We're getting there by co-operating for a change!

# Breaking down barriers

'The major obstacle is the nature of the secondary school curriculum; it is fractured into subjects' (Deputy Head-teacher, West Yorkshire). How can a more holistic curriculum and more holistic working relationships be built up within an institution earlier described as an 'engine house of fragmentationalism'?

Many schools have seen the first step towards a more holistic curriculum as being to bring teams of related disciplines together. However teams do not miraculously gel out of nothing; such changes can be quite 'bloody' with colleagues who cannot accommodate to the new situation leaving the school to be replaced with new, more 'attuned', appointments.

*'I took over the humanities syllabus in 1981 and said to colleagues: "Let's make a list of what we think it is import-ant that students should leave school with at age sixteen, forgetting subject boundaries". It didn't get off the ground until '83/'84; there was a lot of opposition and several people left the department.'*
*(Secondary Head of Humanities, Bradford)*

---

*I would like to see science going more towards bringing in social implications, more questioning and looking at resource material like we have done to a small extent. Obviously there has to be a certain amount of practical work and there has to be certain content, but I would rather see the content reduced, so as to spend time on what I consider more important issues; on relationships between each other and relationships between countries, energy requirements, leading to the whole economic area as well. I think you can have a scientific method of looking at economics, understanding money – Brazilian debt to the Third World banks, I think you could look at that scientifically. That is what you're trying to develop; the danger is that you overlap so much in different areas. I would rather see that coming in than go through some of the rather dry experiments that we have to do, that I have a responsibility to teach because they're on the curriculum and that's what they're going to be assessed on.*

– Secondary Head of Physics, North Tyneside

---

As indicated earlier, the process of developing interdisciplinary team-planned and/or team-taught courses may often turn out to be simply one of exchanging lots of smaller fragments for fewer but larger fragments. The end result still falls short of the holistic. Some schools have, in consequence, begun to experiment with more organic ways of working involving flexible and regroupable cross-curricular teams.

*'It was a happy school but a little bit provincial. It desperately needed a mind-blowing exercise. We made visits to open our minds and learn. Thirty people coming back brainstorming on what they had learnt. A very inspirational time. The timing of it was important to come from the staff, and it indeed came at a very good time after I'd been here a year and a term when I said at a staff meeting: "Right, here's a blank sheet of A4, I want you all to sit in your teams of five and write down what you would love to put in a fourth-year curriculum," and I said that, "No longer do you ever need to say that the exam syllabus is constraining us because this is a fantastic opportunity. We've got a real change now – parents know that there's a GCSE change – so write down with enthusiasm what you really want to do." People do best obviously what they love, so that's the way we started. The deputy head then developed the structuring of it: a ten-day timetable, 100% core, three one and a half hour slots per day and ten curriculum strands. We made a policy that we would try and have teachers teaching in two, three or even four strands.'*
(Secondary Headteacher, Devon)

*'I'd quite like to look at organic structures, where you can put a very small number of people together across a departmental boundary – as few as two, one from each department, who can co-operate on something, then you can always use that for organic growth. . . . Someone was telling me this morning that one of the Humanities teachers and one of the Science teachers have decided to co-operate on soils. We've got an environmental unit in second year Humanities and in science so they've planned it together. We still haven't got far enough to do much in the way of joint planning between the departments. We've got to look for some fairly simple procedures to get that going, and then we will have some organic growth.'*
(Secondary Deputy Headteacher, Leeds)

TVEI extension and modularisation were regularly mentioned as potential ways of fomenting organic change and of introducing a global perspective across the upper secondary school.

*'It may vary according to the institution but clearly the issues world studies is addressing – environmental issues,*

*human rights issues, development issues – will have to be present in the core curriculum of TVEI extension.'*
(Senior Secondary Adviser)

Cross-curricular special events can provide a springboard for greater co-operation and co-ordination between secondary departments and for the more effective permeation of global themes. One secondary school we visited holds an annual 'Development Education Week'. The event, originally inspired by the geography department, has encouraged the English, drama and modern languages departments to regularly take up development themes. Another school was in process of planning an 'Environment Week' which, some hoped, would lead to linked work between science, humanities and other departments. 'The hope is that the Environment Week comes off and is a success and that it brings together all the work we're doing in the school and that it will continue from then on. We're intending to have it as an annual event but to hopefully introduce environmental issues more into the curriculum' (Biology Teacher). At a third school, a 'Peace and Justice Week' had been held as a result of pressure from the religious studies department.

*'When we talked to other heads of department we found that everybody was raising these issues but not at the same time. It was nice to be able to concentrate on them from maths right across. We made a big display and a daily newsletter reporting what was going on in different lessons.'*
(Head of Religious Studies).

Removing barriers which prevent open and genuine relationships between colleagues can also be an important step.

*'It was felt previously that the maths department had to be streamed. So who taught the top stream? The most experienced teacher and new teachers got the bottom streams. We needed to equalise the system such that all teachers have more difficulties, but they are the same difficulties, therefore they can share these and start to leave their doors open.'*
(Secondary Headteacher, Bradford)

A crucial aspect in all these initiatives is the degree to which teachers feel they have some ownership of the change process. This point reflects in microcosm the now widely accepted belief that school-based innovation is likely to be more successful than innovation determined and directed by an outside agency.

*'I suppose it's a question of how does change come about.*

*My own view is that curriculum development that is imposed from the top is asking for trouble, that the kind of change you need in a school is the change that teachers themselves perceive as being necessary, and that they have a stake in the development of that process – there's actually something in it for them, because they have been part of it. I think too that staffrooms are places where at best curiosity about what's going on in certain areas of the school leads to a rethink perhaps in other areas about the way they're approaching whatever they're doing.'*
(Secondary Head of Department, Dorset)

*'This was the vision of where I wanted to go, but it was important that the timing should come from the staff. We have enabled such big changes by involving everybody; when it comes about it is their change.'*
(Secondary Headteacher, Devon)

*'It's about management, organisation, psychology – that you have got a real say. So it's got to be that staff can overturn a decision. I have got to listen to what staff say.'*
(Primary Headteacher, Newcastle)

As important as a sense of ownership in effecting and sustaining whole-school change is the development and nurturing of shared values and a shared vision across the staff and the entire school community.

*'I suspect that one of the problems with the school which we heard about in the news yesterday – it's not really for me to pontificate – but I just suspect that they bolted something into the curriculum, to use the modern phrase, and that they hadn't in fact worked out what their fundamental values were. A bit like giving a chemistry set to a youngster who doesn't understand what he's doing. It might work, but, on the other hand, he might blow himself to pieces.'*
*(Secondary Headteacher, Dorset.)*

*'You've got to have high ideals to begin with. If you keep those in mind, you're aspiring to them. Someday you may actually get there. But if you keep your ideas small all the time, you finish up with something at the end of the day which perhaps isn't worth very much.'*
*(Secondary Modern Languages Teacher, Dorset)*

On a more mundane but, nonetheless, important level, space availability, room lay-out and furniture were frequently cited as factors likely to facilitate or obstruct the change process. The headteacher at a Dorset middle school said that interactive learning had been easier to take on board because the school, which had a dwindling popu-

*The cure for this disease is obvious. We need a validated, usable system of human values, values that we can believe in and devote ourselves to because they are true rather than because we are exhorted to 'believe and have faith.' And for the first time in history, many of us feel, such a system ... based squarely upon valid knowledge of the nature of man, of his society and of his works ... may be possible.*
– Abraham Maslow

lation, had plenty of available space. In a Devon secondary school, all the world studies team were regularly using a diversity of teaching and learning styles with the exception of one teacher whose room and furniture did not easily allow for small group organisation.

---

## Case Study 5

## School is a special place

*This case study has been compiled from interviews with seven staff at St. Peter's School, Bournemouth.*

St. Peter's School, Bournemouth, is a two-site Roman Catholic 11–18 voluntary-aided mixed comprehensive with a population of 1400 students. Its catchment area was described by one teacher as 'one of those white highland ghettos that does not see itself as touched by multi-cultural issues'. 'It's an area of immigration,' said a local educationalist. 'A lot of people have moved into Bournemouth and those people very often say they're on the run from the sort of things that are going on in ILEA.' Such views notwithstanding, many members of staff conceive of the school as having a multi-cultural population.

*'We would certainly see ourselves as a Euroethnic school if I can coin that phrase. We have very few black students but we did a survey a couple of years ago to find out how many children went home to families where they wouldn't speak English as a rule. We found about 120, because it's a Catholic school and we have a lot of Italians, Spaniards, a few Portuguese, that kind of Mediterranean variety.'*
(Anthony MacNamara, Head of English)

A group of staff – from the English and religious education departments – volunteered to join the Dorset world studies in-service programme in 1987/8. The two residential weekends had a profound effect.

*'The world studies weekends generated an enormous amount of discussion amongst ourselves because of the intensity of the experience. They certainly acted as a catalyst. World studies crystallized a number of things for us. It gave us terms of reference to point to, and that's what we didn't have; we didn't have a sense of the totality of what was going on at all and hadn't attempted to put a number of diverse strands in our development into some kind of whole.'*
(Anthony MacNamara)

The world studies weekends triggered 'extensive experimentation' in English classrooms and the drama studio and confirmed members of the R. E. Department in their commitment to tackling controversial social topics. The Headteacher, Brother Bernard Hayward, saw members of the world studies group as key change agents in the school's development of global and multicultural perspectives across the curriculum.

Nicholas Gossip

*'Third year students re-enact a moment of injustice, as experienced by one student. Work in the drama studio helps students to empathise with some injustices felt by characters featured in the novel,* Roll of Thunder, Hear My Cry, *by Mildred Taylor, which is being studied in English lessons.'*

*'Within the school a crucial enabling factor will be those members of staff who have by choice become involved in the county world studies initiative. We will particularly rely on these for the animation of the rest of the staff – for involving them, informing them and enthusing them.'*

To ensure that the initiative doesn't die because of lack of leadership or encouragement from the top, Brother Bernard and one of his senior staff had joined a Southampton University course on multi-cultural education. His hope was that in subsequent years teachers from other departments – he cited history, geography, science and maths as examples – would join the LEA's world studies course. For that to happen, argued Senior Teacher, Kevin Allen, those who had already attended the course needed to do some crucial groundwork by disseminating information, by helping other departments to see the implications of world studies and by prompting them to 'look at how the department may well have to be changed in order to take on board the issues.' From discussions with teachers who had been on the world studies course, it became clear that allies were being carefully cultivated across the school.

*'We have a discussion group that we've set up recently where about a dozen members of staff, half from the sciences and half from the humanities, meet together to discuss a particular topic at somebody's house. Last Friday the topic was ecology and I was enormously impressed by the contribution made by the Head of Biology and the Head of Physics. Those two people, they're on our wavelength without any question or doubt.'*
(Anthony MacNamara)

*'Exchanges of ideas are so important. We have liaised with the history department. There may be a possibility of co-operating with the history department on a project.'*
(Anne McKinney, Teacher of English and Drama)

Amongst most of the seven staff interviewed, there was the feeling that a Roman Catholic school provided a very appropriate context for the introduction of global and multi-cultural education not least because of the firm line taken by the Bishops on issues of race, peace and justice.

*'Within the Catholic syllabus we are actually called upon to tackle what may be considered controversial issues as part of our religious course. We look at the Third World and we also do work which ties in with socially deprived people. In the second year we do a lot of work on the Gospels and in particular we look at Luke's Gospel which presents Jesus almost like a social worker. He's out to help the oppressed in society and this leads us on to work about who we consider society rejects. . . . The guidelines in our R. E. syllabus are very clear that racial prejudice in any form is not to be condoned or approved.'*
(Anne Russell, Teacher of Religious Education)

*'The Church has a strong position on tackling racism in schools. Look at the document* Learning from Diversity. The Challenge for Catholic Education.[2] *. . . Our bishops have also encouraged us to look at global issues and conflict avoidance and resolution in the classroom.'*
(Anthony MacNamara)

*'Our support is contained in the gospels which continually express the value of the individual and multi-cultural education is a vehicle for raising pupils' self-esteem.'*
(Kevin Allen)

Whilst accepting the advantages that being a Catholic school brought to the change processes underway, Brother Bernard also saw disadvantages.

*'Maybe we do have a head start though I am not one hundred per cent sure of that. On the one hand it is true that we have a fairly strong body of opinion within the Catholic Church at the moment, which is undoubtedly looking forward and tackling these many issues honestly and from a genuinely Christian point of view. On the other hand, there is a tendency for practising Catholics and probably practising Christians to be rather conservative and even more sensitive to certain issues. So I am not quite sure which side of the balance we come out on but I would like to think that as a Christian school, with a body of parents many of whom are practising Christians, there would be receptivity to these notions. I do think that there is a trust that parents give to us – they may give it to other schools as well – because we have a number of fundamental principles which they know we are going to stick to.'*
(Brother Bernard Hayward)

The visitor to St. Peter's has the sense of entering a very special place.

*'There are a lot of people who come to this school, who walk through the gate and just say they know it's there; they can't describe sometimes what it is, but they know it's there. It's the same feeling that parents have, new staff, visitors, whatever.'*
(Peter Hartley, Director of Studies)

Contributing to that special atmosphere is a strong sense of shared values pervading the school. The staff had jointly produced a statement of values out of a thorough process of discussion and reflection.

'The only thing that we've done so far is to examine very carefully the philosophy and the values which are the foundation of our own Christian school, and we have written those down carefully and in some detail, and we were very encouraged to find that many of the issues we're now talking about flow naturally from that philosophy, from the values which we find we must support, even treasure, as our livelihood at St. Peter's School.'
(Brother Bernard Hayward)

Special, too, was the wide acknowledgement we found of the multi-dimensional, multi-layered nature of change within a framework of shared values. Change could – and should – come from any quarter, the senior management's role being one of cultivating and supporting initiatives, of linking the islands of change together.

'Interest in world studies has come up from the grassroots; it's not something that has been fed down. I think there are a number of key members of staff who are very sensitive to these issues.'
(Peter Hartley)

'That's my understanding of how change works, that people become interested, that an idea is established as having legitimacy and value, that the people who are working on it, through their enthusiasm, through the fact that they've had a stake in developing it from the beginning and are not doing it because it's imposed, makes it something much more real.'
(Anthony MacNamara)

'I would prefer to see us actually picking up specific initiatives which begin to involve different members of staff, drawing these together to form a coherent picture and then using that as the basis for writing a coherent policy.'
(Brother Bernard Hayward)

There were a number of initiatives, some of long standing, with which the teachers promoting world studies could form a natural alliance. These initiatives themselves contributed very significantly to the special atmosphere of the school and, perhaps, to the special relationship shared with parents.

'Brother Lionel is an ex-teacher of St. Peters. He went to South India eighteen years ago. He works with the poorest of the poor. The school supports him through daily collections and special efforts. Our target every year is £5,000. The money goes straight to him. He writes letters and these get circulated to pupils, parents and parishioners., so if you like we are getting a direct letter every month and that is part of our multicultural education.'
(Peter Hartley)

'This school year has seen the arrival of a new band of merry and enthusiastic lower sixth formers to Dr. Hartley's Amnesty International Group. Since September '87 we have been involved in a number of campaigns. These include writing to the Haitian government about prisoners of conscience, followed by the Syrian Campaign concerning treatment of prisoners, and recently we wrote to the British Home Office about the treatment of refugees arriving in Great Britain.'
(Extract from St. Peter's School Newsletter, no. 24, Spring Term, 1988)

'The Tools for Self Reliance group sends tools to East Africa. The tools are prepared here; if possible we send them off directly, if not we send them to a big workshop on Southampton Water.'
(Peter Hartley)

Brother Bernard hoped that the school would arrive at a policy on global and multicultural education in the not too distant future. 'We cannot feel confident that we're doing something about it until we've actually got something written down.' The policy would be worked out through a process of consultation, moving out from the enthusiasts and seeking to convert the doubters. The change process as far as the staff was concerned he saw very clearly. He was less sure about how students and parents, however, supportive, could be thoroughly involved.

'The school has not worked out how students are going to be involved in the corporate discussion of change. Nor do we have any strategy formulated yet for systematically involving parents and that is a big worry. There is an ad hoc approach and there is the indirect approach through what youngsters tell their parents, but if I was to be told that wasn't very satisfactory I would have to agree.'
(Brother Bernard Hayward)

## Going public on change

*'I'm presenting a paper to the next governor's meeting on what we've been doing and I wanted the staff to agree a statement of intent that the school would pursue the following policies of fairness, etc., etc., and one said: "Well, that's what we're about anyway, aren't we?". So I said: "Yes, but I'd just like to have it written in so that other people know we're about it."'*
(Middle School Headteacher, Dorset)

The formulation of a written school policy was felt to be a critical part of the change process by several of the teachers and headteachers we interviewed. A written policy could legitimise ongoing developments in the school. Timing and the procedures whereby the policy was arrived at were, however, of crucial importance. 'Top downwards' promulgation was universally held to be counter-productive; if staff were not receptive, the policy would stand little chance of being widely acted upon. It was important for staff to be fully consulted so they had a personal commitment to the end-product. That process would itself consolidate the internalisation of a set of shared values across the staffroom.

*'One very important point about any such policy is undoubtedly that one cannot simply sit down in a corner with two or three members of staff, write it, then present it to the*

*staff and say: "Here we are, here's a policy on multi-cultural education, here's a policy on environmental education, here's a policy on health education," because that will simply fall flat on its face. So we see at first very, very important the need for that initial group of enthused, inspired teachers to start involving more and more members of staff in, I think, a sort of gradual process. For example, on the multi-cultural issue alone, we have a lot of converting to do, because there are still a number of staff who are (I don't say this arrogantly) in the position I was a few years ago. So we will have, first of all, a fundamental conversion job to do.'*
(Secondary Headteacher, Dorset)

*'It would be the teacher in charge of world studies' responsibility to lead the staff in the production of a statement. It would be how we've worked in the past on draft statements, either curriculum groups, or one person producing a statement which is presented to the staff, discussed with the staff, amended, in some cases put into practice, and then reported back on, assessed and evaluated and after that, is this fitting the bill or does it need further modification?'*
(Junior Headteacher, Newcastle)

A clear and well-publicised policy can generate parental interest and also help clarify for parents where the school stands on baseline values such as justice, peace, rights and equality. It can also provide teachers with clear guidelines for handling controversial issues. In our visits to schools, however, we came across no example of widespread consultation with parents and the community prior to the promulgation of policy. Likewise, despite the emphasis on participation and openness in world studies and related fields, we found few examples of parents being consulted during the formative stages of the change process in schools (see Case Study 3 for an example of consistent parental consultation and Case Study 6 for another interesting example of parental involvement). Where parents had been involved, the tendency was to invite parents in for a special meeting or evening of activities once practice had become fairly well established.

*'If you are in the engine room, you may not want to know about the icebergs out there.'*
(Secondary Headteacher, Devon)

*'The job still lies ahead of demonstrating to parents that world studies can have a positive impact on a child's basic work.'*
(Middle School Deputy Headteacher, Dorset)

The well-documented case of Groby College, Leicester-shire, where the decision to implement or not to implement a core world studies course hung on parental reactions as culled by neutral observers following a staff presentation and consultation evening has, it seems, rarely been dupli-cated in recent years. It remains one of the few cases, too, of parental suggestions for amendments actually being taken into the proposed syllabus.[3]

*'It's useless just slapping something in front of our youngsters and saying: "Here it is, ready, now get on and eat it." '*
(Secondary Headteacher, Dorset)

As we saw earlier, students can play an important part in the change process in that their enthusiasm and visible change in attitudes and behaviours can help convince teach-ers of the validity of the initiative taken up by colleagues. There is also good evidence of students nurturing and pro-moting change in which they have been actively involved.

*'The fact that the children have done all the work (in the wildlife area and garden) means that they respect what they've done and so we get very little in the way of vandal-ism. We've got five nest boxes on the site and in two of them families of blue-tits were raised and we've had no problems with any vandalism or children going and peering in. They made the nest boxes; it's their school; they respect it.'*
(Middle School Deputy Headteacher, Leeds)

*'The students who were the first guinea pigs were used as ambassadors. If we did a "roadshow" at a primary school, we would take the fourth year, also when visitors came in they would talk to students. It culminated in six of them doing a curriculum presentation to the Education Commit-tee at County Hall.'*
(Secondary Inset Co-ordinator, Devon)

On the other hand, we collected only minimal evidence of students being directly consulted by teachers about any proposed curricular or methodological change. It would seem to us that teachers should have the confidence and strength of their convictions to integrate parents, com-munity members and students more comprehensively in the change process. An holistic view of change demands no less.

An holistic view of change, we also need to remind our-selves, asks us to look beyond the purely institutional con-text and recognise that personal change, the support of the local education authority and its officers and the resources and services of outside agencies are likewise essential elements in the process of transforming schools. Many of the changes described in this chapter have been triggered by teachers who have begun to see the world in new ways as a result of some out-of-school experience.

*'When we came back from the world studies course we were so enthusiastic and we wanted to tell everybody, well at least I did. I felt like I'd been saved. It was that sort of Billy Graham crusading thing and I wanted to tell everybody about it, but I knew that if I went into our staffroom and said: "It was great," they'd all say: "Oh, here she goes again," so I had to sort of curb that, and I discussed it with the headteacher and he said I think we've just got to set an example.'*
(Middle School Headteacher, Dorset)

Many of the teachers have drawn strength from the legitimisation given their work by 'kindred spirits in the advisory service' who have set up courses and projects and provided moral support and sometimes funding for curriculum development initiatives. Others have had the benefit of well-knit networks of local teachers operating under an LEA umbrella and, in some cases, backed by an LEA policy statement. Most have been encouraged or sustained in their work by the materials produced by local and national non-governmental organisations and it is to these organisations that local authority advisers have often turned for the facilitation of in-service training events.

---

## Case Study 6

## What on Earth is World Studies? – Inducting Parents into the Process

*This account of how parents were introduced to a new world studies course at Southway Comprehensive School, Plymouth, is written by Jim Christophers, Co-ordinator for Social Studies.*

The session I have in mind was presented to a group of parents during an evening shortly after we had formally introduced world studies into the upper school (13–16) core curriculum.

The brief was quite straightforward – introducing parents to a change in the curriculum. The execution was rather more complex because the change was not simply one of label (from geography and history to world studies) or simply from option to core but also, and far more

---

significantly, one of approach. It is true that it formed part of a more general process of curriculum development in the school, but this had occurred extremely rapidly and it was bound to be unnerving for the parents of the first cohort of students to experience the new structure.

The Headteacher, with the support of the school's parents' association, arranged for Heads of Department to address parents at a series of evening meetings. The feedback from those attending the previous meetings had been very positive; they had clearly found the information and its presentation interesting and valuable.

But how should we respond? Our curriculum development represented a re-evaluation of the relationships between teachers and students in the learning process and an extension of focus into values and perspectives; the affective dimension of learning and response. Inset we had personally experienced had clearly demonstrated the need to match 'medium and message' and we wanted the parents to experience world studies in a way which would provide opportunities for them to appreciate and understand the basis of our approach rather than merely knowing about the subject.

We accepted the challenge and decided that it was appropriate to move away from the formal didactic style of presentation and relationships usually adopted with parents and to replace this with a participative experience involving genuine personal contact.

The substance of the session is summarised in this statement based on my preparatory notes for the formal input.

'The world impinges on our lives in many ways which are not always immediately apparent to us; as individuals we are members of an interdependent global system and as one element in that system we each have the capacity to produce change within it. The world is shrinking both in terms of the rate of movement of people and in the rate of exchange of ideas and information. The rate at which the world is changing is itself accelerating and within this process so is the capacity for humankind to bring about change. At the same time we are experiencing an unparalleled explosion in the amount of information available and an easing of accessibility to it. This is creating a world which, while it is much more accessible, is increasingly more complex and more difficult to understand. Once it was considered enough simply to know about the world, now it is important for individuals to understand, appreciate and have an involvement with it.

The world is easily distorted because it is viewed not just with one's eyes but with an interpretation that derives from the host of personal experiences and attributes through which we give events and situations meaning. It is reasonable to expect that a range of views will be held on any issues at any scale at any given time and that those views may change over time. If we are to achieve the level of understanding and co-operation which will be required to sustain the planet for the foreseeable future, then we must respect alternative viewpoints and appreciate their nature and origin.'

Within the scenario outlined above it is entirely appropriate that we should approach a study of issues which have global implications in an holistic fashion and taking due cognisance of their aesthetic, emotional and ethical elements.

This in turn suggests an integrated, experiential and reflective approach to learning.

The programme outlined below reflects these considerations and, by changing pace and style, seeks to facilitate a real and positive social experience.

### Programme Summary
*Venue: School Library (comfortable, relaxed)*
*Time: evening*

| *Activity* | *Comment* |
|---|---|
| Affirmation<br>Moving and greeting; Reacting to statements, *Rainstorm* (see Pike & Selby, 1988, 106, for *Rainstorm*) | Simple, short activities were used which immediately began to address alternative points of view in a sometimes humourous context. It set the mood for the whole programme. |
| Fable: *History of a Day* (see Richardson, R., 1979, 59) | Read by a colleague, this introduced a complete change of pace and atmosphere. This fable clearly addresses itself to the pace and nature of change and is controversial enough to be challenging. |
| *Globingo* (see Pike & Selby, 1988, 113) | We restricted this to the standard version because of constraints of time. It proved a very productive introduction to global relationships and had a personal context. |
| OHP illustration of 'The Shrinking World' (see Pike & Selby, 1988, 13, for a suggestion) | Another change in presentation which raised eyebrows as well as a discussion of implications. |
| Analysis of previous day's 9 o'clock news bulletin | I presented a table:<br><br>*Location      Event      Relevance for us*<br><br>By uncovering the location and seeking the rest of the information from the group we enjoyed friendly argument as well as a raising of awareness and understanding. |
| Input | A period of purposeful reflection over the introductory activities. This was extended quite naturally into a presentation of the structuring of the course which would seek to present and explore world studies with the students. Much of this information was given on printed sheets. |

| Activity | Comment |
|---|---|
| Diamond Ranking Exercise: Britain and the Bomb (Statements obtained from Turner, J., 1983; for *Diamond Ranking*, see Pike & Selby, 1988, 134) | This is a major activity which explicitly confronts alternative points of view in a way which avoids indoctrination. The issue is controversial but I felt that it was important to show at least one way in which such areas could be examined. It proved to be remarkably successful and totally absorbing. (Coffee was taken *during* this activity!) |
| Fable: *The Maligned Wolf* (see Pike & Selby, 1988, 53) | Read by a colleague, this provided the perfect ending. The pace and atmosphere was relaxed but the purpose and interest was maintained. |
| Reflection | A general concluding session which lasted longer for some than others and gave an opportunity for the purposes of the programme to be reinforced and for other issues, even fears, to be raised. |

I feel that our approach to the session was justified not just because of the favourable reaction of the parents involved but because I am confident that, by being involved in a participative programme of experiential and reflective learning, they had acquired a deeper understanding of part of the school curriculum than they would have done from a formal presentation.

What next? This is the logical question. For us, I am afraid, it was GCSE with its formative and summative profiling, orals and criterion-referenced assessment. Nothing we could complain about because, along with teachers at other Devon schools, we were responsible for writing them into the scheme. Time consuming nonetheless! Evaluation and revision have taken us into another phase in this development.

We are probably just about ready to go back to our parents again firstly in a general way, as we did before, but then, possibly via the community adult education programme, into a more considered examination of development, environment, peace and human rights (see Greig, Pike and Selby, 1987, 29). But, wait, just a minute, what about the National Curriculum, TVEI, the reactions of SEAC to integrated and modular courses. . . ?

# References

Greig, S., Pike, G & Selby, D., *Earthrights, Education as if the Planet Really Mattered*, Kogan Page/World Wide Fund for Nature, 1987.

Pike, G., & Selby D., *Global Teacher, Global Learner,* Hodder & Stoughton, 1988.

Richardson, R., *Learning for a Change in World Society; Reflections, Activities and Resources*, World Studies Project, 1979.

Turner, J., *The Arms Race*, Cambridge University Press, 1983.

# Case Study 7

# Caught Between the Devil and the Deep Blue 'C'

*Inevitably, some teachers raised the issue of formal assessment as a factor inhibiting change towards holistic education. In this piece, Richard Hedge, Curriculum Co-ordinator, Bridgewater School, Stantonbury Campus, Milton Keynes, discusses the dilemma posed by examinations and identifies forms of assessment most in accord with holistic learning processes.*

'The purpose of schools', wrote one of my students last week, 'is to help you do as well as possible in examinations like GCSE.' Much as we may regret this analysis of our function, it must be clear to all of us involved in state education in Britain that externally scrutinised assessment is set to play an increasing part in our students' lives over the next decade. For those of us trying to explore new approaches to learning, the challenge of developing student-friendly styles of assessment has never been more urgent.

This presents us with a dilemma. For as our understanding of the learning experience we wish to offer our students has developed, so has our awareness that the requirements of external programmes of assessment often impose conditions which militate against the processes we are trying to encourage. The diagram below attempts to summarise aspects of this contradiction. It also attempts to identify how closely seven kinds of assessment activity match up to some of the characteristics of holistic learning.

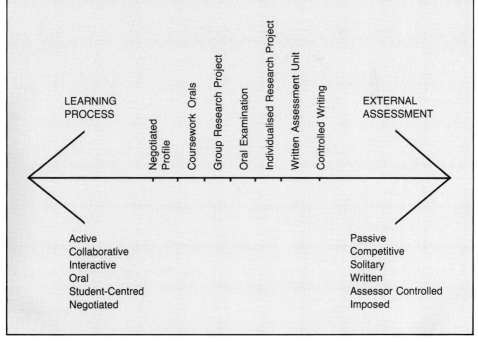

To start at the extreme right of the diagram, by 'controlled writing' I have in mind any piece of written work conducted under rigorous conditions imposed by the teacher. Typically these may include prohibitions on conferring, on asking questions and on consulting reference sources – indeed on many of the processes we are normally most anxious to promote!

This mode of assessment – although a common component of many coursework packages – is profoundly limited by three characteristics: its individuality, its commonality and its irrelevance. The notion of students working on their own at the same imposed task, using the same resources and receiving the same amount of help must surely fill us with alarm. The fact that the skills they are often called upon to use in these units are in some way divorced from any conceivable involvement in real world issues is even more worrying.

Some of these concerns are alleviated by individual research projects. Here students are much more actively in control of their work. They do have the opportunity to interact with a variety of other people. There is far more scope for the task to suit the needs of individual students. And yet the experience is still that of working as an individual in competition with other individuals and the outcome is often almost entirely written. Perhaps most importantly, the demands that this way of working make on time for individualised support are often incapable of being met, leaving students with a sense of dissatisfaction.

In an effort to explore more interactive oral-based approaches to asssessment, some of us have experimented with the use of an oral examination. This is a feature, for example of the Southern Examining Group's World Studies GCSE. Typically, this exam has involved students preparing a short talk on a global issue on which they have strong views and then discussing their opinions with the examiner who will invariably challenge and probe their position. These encounters have often proved memorable for teachers and students alike and have the great advantage of taking a form, in the discussion phase at least, which comes close to replicating real life modes of engagement in issues. A further strength is the flexibility which the interviews give to the teacher to vary the depth, range and subject matter of the conversation according to the interest and ability of the student. Once again, however, there must be concerns about the individualistic and competitive nature of the task and, perhaps more importantly, questions need to be asked about the value of oral exams bolted on to the end of a course if they do not fully represent the kind of interaction that has typified the earlier classroom process.

The three activities at the 'process' end of the continuum have in common an attempt to address the need for collaborative approaches to assessment which are fully integrated into the classroom process. The group research project offers major organisational advantages as well as providing students with the opportunity to work within a co-operative framework in ways which are suited to their own strengths and weaknesses. This kind of project is often a feature of humanities coursework packages and is an institutionalised part of the SEG World Studies scheme. The groupwork unit in this scheme also requires students to reflect on their own roles within the group and to comment on the processes of interaction and co-operation which have (usually!) taken place. This is a demanding experience for many adolescents but one which has put the emphasis on their roles as partners rather than competitors. Some of this focus has, however, been diffused by the exam board requirement, common to all such group activities, that recognisable individual contributions are available for moderation.

Coursework oral assessments were a part of the original South West Examining Board's CSE in World Studies and are an integral part of GCSE English schemes. They can be genuinely interactive, characteristically involving groups of 4–6 students working together. Perhaps their greatest advantage over any of the activities described above is the fact that they flow more naturally from the learning processes within an holistic classroom and thus allow for assessment which is genuinely continuous. They also allow students to demonstrate their abilities in a much wider range of contexts including discussion, debate, role play and problem-solving activities.

Taking this integration of assessment and classroom process a stage further, the SEG World Studies scheme also includes a negotiated profile in which student and teacher meet on five occasions during the course to reflect on the student's progress across the whole range of learning activities. This gives scope for recognition of students' contributions in and out of the classroom – including, for example, participation in first hand research or community action which may be difficult to acknowledge in other ways. It also allows the students to play an active role in evaluating their own progress and an opportunity to comment on and, perhaps, challenge assessments made by the teacher. Clearly, the requirements of formal assessment mean that the teacher has the final word on grading but the discussion and occasional disagreement which precede this point are invariably educative for both parties. It must be said that not all students find this process of self reflection and evaluation an easy one and, for some their powers of expression are stretched to the limit. The following excerpts from the final review session of a far from able student, however, perhaps serve to illustrate what she has gained from both the course as a whole and the profiling process in particular:

Student: *All through my world studies course I found it reasonable because some topics that we learnt about I didn't know nothing about but now I have a slight understanding of some topics. I quite enjoyed the course . . . I found it much easier when we did groupwork.*

Teacher: *Alison has gained more from this course than any examination grade will indicate. She has clearly improved her knowledge of a number of world issues and at the same time she has developed a number of personal qualities, especially relating to small groupwork.*

# References

1. Harland, J., & Weston, P., *Living with Uncertainty: Professional Development in the Lower Attaining Pupils Programme*, NFER, mimeo, undated.

2. *Learning from Diversity. The Challenge for Catholic Education*, report of the Working Party on Catholic Education in a Multiracial and Multicultural Society, Catholic Media Office, July 1984.

3. Aucott, J., Cox, H., Dodds, A., & Selby, D. E., 'World Studies on the Runway: One Year's Progress Towards a Core Curriculum', *The New Era*, vol. 60, 6, November/December 1979, 212–29.

I've sat on a stone fence about a great, soft, sloping field
of musing heifers, a farmstead
slanting its planes calmly in the calm light
a dead elm raising bleached arms
above a green so dense with life –
slugs, moles, pheasants, gnats, spiders, moths,
hummingbirds, groundhogs, butterflies –
a lifetime is too narrow
to understand it all, beginning with the huge
rockshelves that underlie all that life.

– Adrienne Rich

·CHAPTER FIVE·

# The Local Education Authority and the Change Process

The school is a sub-system within a larger system – the local education authority. Like any sub-system, it exhibits both assertive and integrative tendencies. Whilst self-consciously cultivating its own distinct identity, its culture, its sense of the possible, the directions it takes are influenced in a variety of ways by the system within which it functions. Its working, in turn, subtly affects the nature, ethos and direction of the larger system.

The majority of teachers and educationalists interviewed referred to individual LEA officers as having had a significant influence upon the change process. Open support for global education by two Chief Education Officers (one long-standing, one recently-appointed) was reported to us as having legitimised and stimulated change within their respective authorities.

*'The Chief Education Officer made clear his desire to see the development of world studies. He is a compassionate man with broad views and he felt a global perspective was an important part of the curriculum.'*
(Local University Lecturer in Education)

*'We have had no Director for some time. Now I feel comfortable in terms of what the present Director is saying. I identify strongly with the way he is projecting the views of the authority.'*
(Junior Headteacher)

The appointment of a Principal Adviser was mentioned as a significant landmark in the spread of world studies in one authority. 'Christian and liberal, his personal value system led him to see these issues as vitally important.' (Senior Adviser, Secondary Education). Reference was more regularly made to those in the advisory service holding somewhat less exalted posts who had worked assiduously for curriculum development and the introduction of a greater diversity of teaching and learning styles in schools. Their work was the more effective, it was generally recognised, if they were able to form working alliances with other advisory colleagues.

*'A key enabling factor has been the appointment of a health/ PSE Adviser who has run courses on active learning; also the appointment of a Senior Adviser with very strong views. There have been several other pro-active learning advisory appointments and there are now far more cross-curricular issues coming from the advisory service into the schools.'*
(Middle School Headteacher)

*'I'm very pleased to be able to say that we are now being able to expand because there are kindred spirits in the advisory service. . . . It's a pincer movement in some respects. You cultivate people who've got influence, positions of power within the authority, whether it's in the advisory service, or in a school, and you build from below as well, hoping that the pressure from one or two key people from above will help deliver what you're really after. The strategy has got to include the means of winning over people who've got a responsibility within the advisory service for the middle and the first school phase. I think that's absolutely crucial.'*
(Senior Adviser, Secondary Education)

One tactic for winning support amongst advisory colleagues is to invite them to attend and participate in residential in-service courses. In one LEA, the Secondary Adviser promoting world studies invited his primary counterpart and selected teachers from feeder primary schools to two world studies weekends arranged primarily for secondary teachers. This led directly to world studies curriculum development in some of the primary schools represented. In another, a Senior Secondary Adviser who had developed world studies in one half of the authority managed to firm up the support of an (already sympathetic) colleague with responsibilities in the other half of the county as a result of the latter's attendance at a weekend course. In the next annual round of world studies inset, teachers from both halves of the LEA were represented following enthusiastic canvassing by both advisers.

The in-service course is one of the major catalysts for change open to the adviser. Its effect, as we have seen, can be profound. Four ingredients are crucial to its long-term success. It needs to be *well-planned and well-executed*; there needs to be an *effective aftercare strategy*; its impetus needs to be *sustained* and those attending the course or influenced by developments arising out of the course need to be *networked*.

# Course Planning and Preparation

Selection of schools for participation on in-service courses is of critical importance, especially if the strategy is one of creating exemplars of good practice that begin to attract interest in the authority at large. In one LEA the senior secondary advisor principally involved in promoting world studies has, in each school year since 1986/7, organised a 'World Studies 10–13 Project' involving up to twenty course days and embracing staff from two or more clusters of primary, middle and secondary schools. Teachers from each cluster have attached to them a teacher tutor – a teacher who has attended a previous year's course (the tutors in 1986/7 had attended a three-LEA Joint Regional Course in World Studies in 1985/6).

*'I realise now that the schools I selected initially to go into the project – that that was possibly the toughest patch in the authority for all sorts of reasons – I'm not sorry for that, but I couldn't have started with a tougher patch. We've hung onto that patch, and we're continuing to develop it – we won't let go but, clearly, it has caused us moments of grief.'*
(Senior Adviser, Secondary Education)

Subsequent clusters have been chosen by identifying schools where there are teachers likely to grasp the opportunity of being involved in world studies, where teachers participating in the project are likely to receive strong backing from the senior management and where the ethos of the school is one conducive to change. Having identified the schools, a direct approach is made to the headteacher.

*'We have identified a school where there is a Head of Humanities – which is significant in itself – who is clearly sympathetic to the kinds of concerns tackled by world studies. There is a group that already exists that in a sense is looking for a bit of a "raison d'être" and therefore it's likely to take off, and there is a Head who is supportive of the*

*development. I personally made sure of that. So you could say that we've tried to make sure that all those pieces were in place in deciding on the school that was going to be involved.'*
(Secondary Adviser)

*'We got involved through the Senior Adviser's direct approach, he having judged the school to be ripe for it.'*
(Secondary Headteacher)

An important element in the groundwork for each project year has become the encouragement of senior management representation on the course itself.

*'Where a school has said it will put X number of staff into a curriculum development project, I think as part of that you need to contract a member of staff into that project as a minder if you like, a keeper (a member of the senior management team), so that they can facilitate and develop, be aware of what the issues are and help those members of staff in their relationships with the wider staff of that school. Indeed, I'll go beyond that – I'd like to see those same senior managers tied in with that project so they could actually use their skills from management training and relate it in a direct way to what was going on in curriculum development.'*
(Senior Adviser, Secondary Education)

Another essential part of the project planning process is, clearly, to ensure that the in-service facilitation is of the highest quality. The in-service residential weekend courses on the 'World Studies 10–13 Project' have been led by officers of an external agency and their interactive, participatory style has won the plaudits of teachers and advisers alike. In some instances, in other authorities, we heard of examples where inset events had actually threatened to put the change process into reverse. 'They came back saying, "What a waste of time. They talked for hours. I was bored." It was sad – much more valuable to go in and see Mr. H. and his children enjoying themselves.' (Middle School Headteacher). Ensuring that the inset providers are up to the job is sometimes allowed to be a chancy 'bush telegraph' affair; at best, advisers go and see the prospective facilitators in action before making their final choice.

## Aftercare and Support

Teachers returning from a powerful inset event experience a wide range of emotions. Some are gripped by what might be described as a Messianic urge; some feel a great sense of isolation; some have a feeling of reluctance about returning to what they conceive of as the dull and mundane; some feel a great need for guidance and support as they seek to implement what they have learnt; some feel a mixture of all or most of these things. A second crucial element in the long-term success of a curriculum development programme is *effective post-course aftercare*. 'The high points have been every residential weekend. The low points have been trying to pick up people after the weekend experiences.' (Senior Adviser, Secondary Education). Advisers talked of the strategies at their disposal for supporting teachers on their return to school, such as visiting the school periodically to talk with the individual or team concerned and arranging a meeting attended by the course members, the senior management and themselves. The problems were those of time and the excessive demands made upon the advisory service.

*'It is not the facilitators' role to prepare people for the tough time back in school. The authority ought to be doing that because we know the patch best and we should have the answers and the strategies and the rest properly mapped out. I think we're making progress, but I can't pretend that we've given it the degree of time and attention we should have done. In a sense I'm apologising, but I'm also saying that the demands on me, for example, and the nature of the tasks I have to do, in the end make it very much a compromise situation. I have to be realistic about what is possible. I am more optimistic now because I feel I've got support and colleagues around me who can begin to really tackle these issues probably more systematically than I've done.'*
(Senior Adviser, Secondary Education)

In the case of the 'World Studies 10–13 Project' described earlier, support and aftercare was also provided by the teacher tutors. At each of the two residential weekends (November and February), time was allotted for tutors to meet their clusters and then plan for work back in school. At the second weekend, time was additionally set aside for teachers to share successes they had enjoyed and problems they had encountered. The tutors had been released from school for one afternoon each week throughout the school year to visit the teachers involved in the project for the purposes of discussing progress, planning lessons and team teaching. 'The three teacher tutors have been crucial, pushing an impetus and enthusiasm which wouldn't be achieved if it was just coming from the teachers and the advisers.' (Secondary Adviser). Also built into the programme were periodic cluster meetings for joint planning and evaluation purposes, visits to schools inside and outside the authority by cluster teams to see world studies in action in the classroom and additional inset days on particular themes. In another local education authority, the officers of the external agency facilitating the two residential weekends (November and June) were hired in as in-school consultants, their brief being to visit schools involved to discuss progress and plan courses with teachers and also to offer guidance on classroom activities and resources. Their work also involved keeping the adviser with responsibility for world studies abreast of developments.

---

*'One-off' courses are inadequate for real change. In order to tackle such problems as 'burn-out' and 'de-skilling' a professional development strategy is needed which recognizes that change is a long-term process. Projects have employed a number of strategies for longer term support: central teams working with schools, support teachers attached to schools on contract, securing time for project staff to meet together regularly in school, school-based secondments for one or more days a week over a term or a year. There is a need, though, to provide support for the full life of the initiative and to ensure that the time of any release allows teachers to interweave practice and critical reflection, with the assistance of colleagues of appropriate expertise. Sustained support does require a clear allocation of responsibility for overall planning throughout the life of the project.*

– John Harland & Penelope Weston

---

Teacher secondment has been used by some local authorities as a means of promoting change whilst at the same time providing teachers with the necessary support. In one LEA, a teacher was seconded to act as the link-person between the authority and a university centre involved in the promotion of global education. The teacher used his time at the centre to familiarise himself with the latest classroom activities and reources and to hone his in-service facilitation skills. A major part of his secondment was, however, spent in the authority running short inset courses and providing back-up for teachers. In a second LEA, a teacher who had developed a 'Spaceship Earth' course for middle school years spent most of his secondment promoting, supporting and evaluating its use in a range of primary and secondary schools in the authority. Secondments for shorter periods can also be very effective (see Case Study 9). Such developments would not have taken place save for the perspicacity of an adviser who recognised the change agency potential of the individual teacher concerned. We came across the odd instance of teachers who had made a signal contribution to curriculum development and/or whole school change being completely overlooked by their advisory service.

*'I'm disappointed that the Adviser hasn't been interested enough to come in and look at the work. . . . Unless the adviser sees the work, then our area of influence will remain within this community.'*
(Infant Headteacher)

*'The advisory service has never taken up Mr H. as an exemplar. The service has no impact on schools. There is nobody responsible for middle school education. No Environmental Studies Adviser. Mr W. was very good but he's now retired. He knew the staff and was respected. Things were just beginning when he left.'*
(Middle School Headteacher)

## Sustaining the Change Process

To illustrate the importance of *sustained* inset and support, let us outline developments in Newcastle LEA in the last few years. In the city a world studies curriculum development group was established as a result of a number of one-day conferences held in 1982/3 by the Schools Council World Studies 8–13 Project. In October 1984 members of the group were encouraged by the LEA to attend a weekend residential course organised by the World Studies Northern Regional Group and facilitated by staff of the then World Studies Teacher Training Centre, York University (now the Centre for Global Education). As a result of this experience, the curriculum development group organised six evening workshops for primary teachers in January and February 1985. In 1985/6 a member of the group was seconded to the Centre for Global Education (CGE) to work towards a Diploma in Global and Multicultural Education. The teacher concerned spent much of the year developing her skills as an in-service trainer, in which role the authority has from time to time used her. In 1986/7 two separate world studies groups were established within the authority both working under consultancy arrangements with CGE. 'Newcastle 1' was 'a pilot group of twelve schools (nine primary, two middle, one secondary) stragegically situated across the city so that further development could be centred on those schools.'[1] 'Newcastle 2' was a group of teachers in the Walker district of Newcastle co-ordinated by the Head of Walker Lower Secondary

School (on a year's secondment). Each term a different teacher from each of the four feeder primary schools was seconded to work with the co-ordinator on the development and trial of a range of activities on a particular world studies theme. The resulting handbook, *Co-operating for a Change*[2], has been widely taken up and used by teachers across the authority (see Case Studies 4 and 9). In 1987/8 and 1988/9 further inset and consultancy arrangements were made with CGE so as to maintain the momentum of change in those schools in the authority already committed to world studies. As before, the consultancies involved a mixture of residential in-service weekends and regular visits to schools. This brief history gives some indication of the level of personal, organisational and financial commitment involved in fomenting and consolidating a major curriculum change in one authority.

*No man is an Island, entire of itself; every man is a piece of the Continent, a part of the main. . . . Any man's death diminishes me, because I am involved in Mankind; And therefore never send to know for whom the bell tolls; it tolls for thee.*
– John Donne

In Newcastle a 'twilight' session for teachers involved in world studies is held at a local teachers' centre generally on the first Monday of each month. Each meeting is devoted to a particular topic but a valuable opportunity is also there for teachers belonging to various schools and initiatives to simply meet and share experiences. The chance to *network* is important in sustaining change, whether the network takes the form of periodic meetings, an occasional newsletter or irregular letters and telephone conversations between teachers. One Secondary Adviser in another authority talked of the needs for 'a support mechanism whereby a group reconvenes from time to time.' It was important to 'simply give people the opportunity to be together with people from the other side of the county who have been involved in the development so far.' Such networks can, of course, also feed into and feed from larger, regional or national, networks linking those active in global education and related fields.

Alerting the 'conspirators' to each other's work, connecting seemingly separate islands of growth and development, it has been suggested at several points in this book, is a crucial element in achieving the critical mass necessary for social transformation. At the local education authority level, as important as networking individuals, is the task of linking initiatives that share mutual or overlapping goals and philosophies. In Newcastle, the advisory service has sought to connect world studies developments with initiatives arising out of the authority's policy commitments on race and gender. In Dorset, members of the advisory service have been at pains to link ongoing world studies and multicultural education initiatives. In a small number of schools senior management have been encouraged to attend a multi-cultural education course at Southampton University, whilst other staff members have been attached to the world studies inset course. The teams returning from the two courses have been able to pool experiences: the more theoretically-oriented multi-cultural course providing ideas in such areas as the development of school policies and textbook evaluation; the world studies course feeding directly into the practical classroom situation. Links are also being sought with the authority's Learning for a Changing World (LFCW) Project. The Project, partly funded by BP Educational Liaison, seeks to develop pre-vocational courses delivered across the curriculum and aimed at giving students 'of all abilities aged 11–16 a better opportunity to become economically literate, technologically capable and prepared for adult and working life.' A document prepared by advisers overviewing the Project draws extensively upon world studies: 'World Studies has addressed a number of important cross-curricular dimensions – the multicultural nature of society, (the) complex interdependent world, the environment, education for democracy and human rights'; 'World Studies has always recognised the pivotal importance of catering for the range of preferred learning styles to be found in any one classroom''. It also points out that 'advances in both the arts and sciences in the twentieth

*Sitting Circle. Dorset teachers end a workshop session on interdependence by putting the principle into practice.*

Vic Fowler

century have sharpened our awareness of the inter-related-ness of all phenomena' and that 'we need to emphasise lessons learnt from World Studies (and LFCW) Projects as to the importance of interdisciplinarity as the best prep-aration for a world of change.' The multicultural, world studies and LFCW initiatives have also been linked to a cumulative programme of inset workshops exploring teach-ing and learning style theory and its classroom and school implications. Advisers, secondary headteachers and deputy headteachers have attended workshops and, each year, newly-qualified teachers now receive a two-day introduc-tion to teaching and learning style theory as part of their probationary programme. Plans are also now well advanced for linking the four developments so far described to the authority's TVEI extension programme.

## Case Study 8

### World Studies in Devon

*This case study draws upon an interview with Bryan Stephenson, a key figure in the develop-ment of world studies in Devon and, until recently, a Lecturer in Education at the University of Exeter. It also takes extracts from Bryan's article, 'The Growth of World Studies in Devon' which appeared in* World Studies Journal, *vol. 4, no. 3, Spring 1983, 5–17.*

The beginning of a general awareness in Devon of world studies as a curriculum movement appears to lie in a net of coincidences in the early summer of 1982. An invitation had been made to members of the Humanities Faculty at Groby College, Leicestershire, where there was a World Studies core curriculum for fourth and fifth years, to run a day's programme of lectures, workshops and seminars for secondary teachers at the School of Education, Exeter University. This took place in June 1982. For a significant number of those who met the Groby team in June their work had much appeal. Their visit coincided with the Chief Education Officer's expressed desire to see the development of world studies. Also important was the existence in Devon of a curriculum movement 'Teaching for a World of Limited Natural Resources' (TWLNR). This had led to the production of guidelines and teaching materials which focussed upon the nature of environmental problems and the relationship of these to social, economic and political factors. Richard Westley, County Adviser for Geography and Environmental Edu-cation, was servicing agent to the project. His commitment to TWLNR inclined him to support other initiatives headed in the same direction. In Exmouth, a Centre for International Studies had also been created, one aim of which has been to promote development education within the South West. The Groby visit also coincided with various activities on the part of a peace education group in Devon which was – and still is – a small group which occasionally mushrooms into something larger when it organises an event such as a workshop. There were also one or two teachers very much involved in human rights education. To those who had been involved in more than one of these developments, the attraction of world studies lay in the opportunity it afforded for linking these different yet related perspectives within a more coherent framework.

The desire to alert schools to the need to review their policies with regard to multi-cultural education may be significant in explaining the interest shown by the LEA's senior staff in world studies. It may at the same time have been seen by them as complementing the concurrently developing programme of Social, Personal and Moral Education within the county. Another significant factor was the introduction of the authority's new curriculum staffing policy whereby there was the opportunity for schools to obtain additional staff and to make scale point allocations to facilitate the development of courses in new curriculum areas. One of five such curriculum areas identified by the Chief Education Officer was world studies. The county was, thus, prepared to make money available, there was a county Adviser prepared to give his support and, in addition, I was able to use my contacts to facilitate the development.

Despite earlier contacts with the Schools Council World Studies 8–13 Project, it was thought appropriate to concentrate initial efforts on the older secondary age range. A week-long county in-service course in September 1982 was re-oriented towards world studies as the first contribution to the 'movement'. In facilitating this, David Selby – who had by this time moved from Groby to the World Studies Teacher Training Centre at York University (now the Centre for Global Education) – was able to enlarge on ideas presented in June. It was not surprising that the insights, previous convictions and experiences of participants coalesced into a general wish to disseminate the ideas with which they had been dealing more widely within the county and to secure backing from the LEA for initiatives which they might take within their own schools. This was articulated in a recommendation submitted to the Chief Education Officer through a paper drafted by the combined efforts of course members. The proposals from the September 1982 course did lead to a series of recommendations being put to Devon County Council's Sub-Committee and approved by it in March 1983.

The Centre for International Studies' South West Development Education Project was responsible for the initial proposal for the Joint Regional Course in world studies held in 1983/4. The programme included major contributions from the World Studies Teacher Training Centre. Further Joint Regional Courses, again using the Centre's expertise, were held in 1984/5 and 1985/6. Centre staff also visited schools involved during this period. In the first two years of the world studies 'movement' in Devon much time and effort were given over to the construction of a group Mode 3 CSE syllabus, although there were also schools developing non-examination courses across various age ranges and others which grafted world studies into Personal, Social and Moral Education programmes. The second and third Joint Regional Courses involved primary teachers and two primary groups were established, based in Plymouth and North Devon.

What has happened in the past two years has been a massive investment in the development of a GCSE course which has consumed quite a lot of energy. Where meetings are held on world studies, they are largely based on the GCSE. My own personal prejudices show through here but I've always regretted that world studies took the form of an examination. I argued against it but once the decision on the part of my colleagues in schools was made I was entirely committed. I have to say that were it not for the examination system being developed, world studies would not be talked about as much as it is but it would still be a flag-bearer. The other reservation I have is that we have not been able to establish adequately an 8–13 initiative.

You could argue that we've got to the stage where no-one looks askance when world studies is referred to, because it is established in some schools in the county. That's not to say people aren't suspicious or antipathetic, but there have been publicly organised meetings, supported by the authority, and so one could argue that in a sense these things have become routine. World studies was accepted as a GCSE subject and, whatever its future in that direction, it did become part of the curriculum scene in the 1980s. Whatever misconceptions people have about the nature of world studies – and they are considerable – at least it has become part of the general awareness, part of the language of curriculum development, even though it is still only a minority of schools that have taken it up in a committed fashion.

When does an innovation cease to be an innovation? At what point do you say 'Well, that's there and looking after itself and has become assimilated'? My guess is that, as with most innovations, it's impossible to generalise, but that whilst one accepts that there is quite a bit going on that is not easily detectable, there is also a large area which is unaffected still – many teachers remain solidly committed to practices and ways of thinking which are incompatible with the ideas and approaches of world studies. And there are others who need a good deal of encouragement if they are to have confidence in their abilities to adopt world studies ideas and methods. But, once the money runs out, who follows that up? No-one to my knowledge – the hope is that the initiative will be self-sustaining. The whole question of aftercare is inadequately considered, it's not budgetted for; that's part of the problem.

# LEA Policies: A Note

A local education authority policy statement can provide a powerful legitimising umbrella for curriculum and whole school change. As with school policy statements, gauging the appropriate method and moment for its formulation and promulgation is of critical importance. It seems that a 'head of steam' for change needs to be built up at a variety of levels prior to the publication of the policy otherwise there is every danger of it becoming a dead letter. It is also clear that an authority infrastructure needs to have been established to meet expectations raised by the policy. There is always 'the problem that any widespread curriculum growth can cause, that of the difficulty support-services may have in coping quickly with a new kind of demand.'[3] It is also the case that the most effective policies are ones where those expected to act upon the policy feel they have had some chance of contributing to its development. This was clearly the case when the World Studies Recommendations were put out by Devon Local Education Authority (see Case Study 8). We did not come across any case of widespread parental or student consultation during the formulation of LEA policy.

Advisers in some authorities felt that the nature of the area where they were working precluded any attempt to enact policy that might be seen as promoting the study of controversial issues in the classroom. A discreet approach tacking particular aims and objectives onto more broadly-based statements of policy was, they felt, a surer way forward.

'The idea of having a discrete policy statement on world studies, or on equal opportunities, or on multicultural education, or indeed on political education, I don't think you'll ever see that here. My reading of the political climate is that it will never allow that sort of explicit stand-alone sort of statement which is allowed in other authorities.'
(Senior Adviser, Secondary Education)

The success of LEA strategies to effect and sustain change in schools is reliant upon the commitment of individual teachers and the schools themselves. Teachers who have undergone personal and professional change have a key change agency role in LEA programmes both as nodal points of influence and inset providers. Schools where the 'chemistry' is appropriate for change are equally crucial in that they offer arenas for productive experimentation in the early phases of change and exemplars for other schools to follow as the change process moves forward and spreads out. What occurs in schools – the sub-system – can feed back and influence the behaviour and direction of the larger system.

'I think what world studies has probably done most within the authority is in the whole question of learning style theory. I think there's no question about that – the way that's influenced the practice of the primary team – the fact that they know that through world studies they've actually got a foothold if you like in schools because of two or three staff having been on the world studies course and are conversant with learning style theory and can begin to show other members of staff various learning strategies, that's been probably the most significant thing, and that's clearly affected and influenced the way the primary team functions.'
(Senior Adviser, Secondary Education)

Whilst we found few cases of local and regional non-governmental agencies enjoying formal relationships with local education authorities, it is clear that such organisations have fed into authority-initiated change processes by taking on consultancy/inset roles which the authority is unable to fill with its own officers because of understaffing and, more particularly, by providing the classroom resource materials so crucial to securing a positive response from teachers to the change being promoted.

# References

1. Baker, T., *et al.*, *Co-operating for a Change*, Newcastle upon Tyne LEA, 1987, 1.

2. See note 1. The handbook is available from Cliff Winlow, Education Development Centre, Pendower Hall, West Road, Newcastle NE15 6PP.

3. Stephenson, B., 'The Growth of World Studies in Devon', *World Studies Journal*, vol. 4, no. 3, Spring 1983, 9.

·CHAPTER SIX·

# Change from Without: External Agencies

One of the principal aims of the Global Impact Project was to identify and evaluate the role of external agencies in the promotion of global education in schools, with a view to making recommendations for the development of effective strategies for the 1990s. It was our view that an understanding of change processes in education, and particularly of an holistic model of change, was central to our task. In this chapter we shall explore the evidence we have collected from interviews concerning the function of external agencies and, utilising our understanding of holistic change, suggest where the greatest potential lies for such agencies in the next decade.

The term 'external agencies', as we have used it, covers a wide range of organisations involved in curriculum and professional development; broadly, it includes those which are attempting to promote change in schools towards a more global and holistic education. A questionnaire survey of some 183 local and national agencies was carried out during the first stage of the Global Impact Project.[1] For our in-depth research we concentrated upon selected, locally-based environmental education and development education agencies, all of which had direct links with at least one of the schools where interviews had taken place. In this way we hoped to discover the 'chemistry of contact' between schools and agencies which nurtures global education. Many of these agencies would be classed as 'non-governmental organisations' (NGOs), funded largely from charitable sources or in receipt of governmental funding. Reference will also be found to organisations which receive money from industry and from local education authorities. Some organisations are virtually autonomous in their policymaking, others need to take account of the demands of funding bodies, parent organisations or hosting institutions. Such factors will obviously have some bearing upon an organisation's ability to influence schooling. They nonetheless reflect the present day reality of constraints and possibilities within which agencies have to work, especially if their interests do not lie within the 'mainstream' areas of education. Our aim is not to conclude that any one type of organisation is the most effective, nor any single approach the most productive, but to suggest ways in which all organisations might capitalise upon their potential. Our underlying assumption is that external agencies can make a very important contribution to the process of change towards holistic education.

## Resources for courses

Our task in the first part of the chapter is to establish how external agencies attempt to influence schooling and to explore the perspectives of teachers on the products and services they provide. The most common function of all agencies we surveyed was that of providing curriculum resources on a wide range of global issues. During interviews, most of the major resource-producing organisations concerned with world development and the environment were mentioned by teachers as providing materials relevant for classroom use. Many teachers were full of praise for the quality and appropriateness of these resources.

*'There's a series of books,* Teaching Development Issues[2] – *I picked up one that we had on inspection. I really like the way they're set out for pupils. They are very readable – that's often a problem with this sort of material, if you're not careful, because the issues are 'out there' and pupils can't always identify with 'out there'. You've got to be able to bring it down to something that is easy to understand, and they had lots of ideas and games for this.'*
(Secondary Humanities Teacher, Leeds)

*'Some of the role-play games are very good, for example the Mali Cattle Game – very simple, but very good indeed. Also the Banana Game has gone incredibly well with some groups. These add another dimension.'*
(Secondary Science Teacher, Devon)

From some teachers who spent a lot of time on teaching global issues came almost a sense of greed for 'any good materials I can get hold of' from external agencies, reflect-

*Percentage of respondents ranking the following sources of material according to amount of use when dealing with development/environmental issues.*

| Sources of material | Amount of use | | | |
|---|---|---|---|---|
| | never | some-times | fairly frequently | very frequently |
| national non-governmental organisations | 28 | 48 | 18 | 6 |
| local non-governmental organisations | 31 | 50 | 15 | 4 |
| commercial firms | 33 | 48 | 14 | 6 |
| SCDC/Schools Council | 46 | 40 | 11 | 3 |
| library services | 16 | 37 | 27 | 20 |
| material produced by yourself or by colleagues | 2 | 16 | 33 | 50 |
| museum services | 35 | 36 | 18 | 11 |
| LEA teachers' centres | 25 | 44 | 21 | 10 |
| in-service courses | 23 | 47 | 22 | 8 |
| magazines/journals | 5 | 44 | 36 | 15 |
| newspapers | 8 | 45.5 | 34 | 12.5 |
| educational publishers | 8 | 41 | 29 | 22 |

– Global Impact survey of environmental and development education in schools.

ing the paucity and poor quality of relevant resources from mainstream educational publishers.

*'Yes, we've found useful material that's come from those sources and has been repackaged. In lots of the curriculum units which are available for use in 14–18 or 16–19 age ranges, the materials from OXFAM and other NGOs have been packaged as part of case studies. There's one on water management in the Sahel, there's one on Latin American cities. There's a lot of project work where we use material from these sources. They package them very, very attractively – they have the time and we haven't'.*
(Secondary Geography Teacher, Leeds)

A Devon social studies teacher, who claimed that 'quite a lot of that sort of material is around the school and being used', said that she 'may only use part of a pack' and would 'stress to the children the sources of the material to indicate this is a particular point of view. I aim to give several different perspectives, to develop awareness of several choices and of bias, and encourage children to make judgements themselves.' A science colleague at the same school who used 'a whole file of stuff' from environmental agencies finds that 'the material needs altering sometimes, to remove contentious titles – for example – and just present information as different points of view.' The problem of 'balance' and bias in resources was raised by a number of teachers, as was the difference in standards of presentation.

*'The main problem is that organisations like the Atomic Energy Authority and British Nuclear Fuels have masses of money and produce lots of glossy material. NGOs like Friends of the Earth and the Centre for Alternative Technology can't compete – theirs tends to be on recycled paper. We have to stress to students, "Look at the facts, not the glossiness; try to uncover the truth." '*
(Secondary Physics Teacher, North Tyneside)

A Dorset teacher of 7–9 year olds commented favourably on some of the development agencies' packs.

*'These have been very useful – the ideas can be adapted to suit much younger children. Much of the material is aimed at older children, but this can be very positive in raising expectations and therefore achieving higher standards. Material for this age range is not readily available – you've got to be prepared to go and look for what you want.'*

Here she raises two points echoed by very many teachers: firstly, the dearth of materials produced especially for very young children; secondly, the time-consuming task of discovering what resources are available. Infant teachers, in particular, expressed a need for appropriate resources such as 'packs of glossy pictures, especially colour', simple stories and artefacts. Easier access to resources was an expressed need of primary and secondary teachers alike. 'What we would like is a library here that we would all dip into, because I'm forever scanning books for ideas' (Dorset Middle School Teacher); 'It's an effort to go to the centre because it's a distance away. If there was a store of this stuff in school, it would be used' (Newcastle Primary Teacher); 'I use lots of stuff from the nuclear industry and from environmental groups, although it's never as easy to get hold of as I would expect it to be' (Devon Secondary Teacher). A 'lack of time to research and review resources' was the reason most frequently given for limited use of external agency resources, or for not using them at all.

*Percentage of agencies surveyed producing resources aimed at the following age ranges.*

| Age Range | % |
| --- | --- |
| nursery/infant (4 – 7) | 24 |
| junior (8 – 11) | 51 |
| lower secondary (11 – 13) | 51 |
| middle secondary (14 – 16) | 50 |
| 16+ | 52 |
| adult | 52 |
| community/family groups | 37 |

– Global Impact survey of non-governmental organisations and statutory bodies.

*'I haven't used any other resources – I haven't seen any. I haven't gone out of my way to look for them; you haven't the time to do it. They need to be given into your hand.'* (Primary Teacher, Newcastle)

A North Tyneside Head of Religious Studies who used a lot of development agency materials, admitted to 'spending more time trying to find out what is around, making contacts, testing out material, than I would like to – but it's the only way.' A Leeds biology teacher who incorporated materials from a wide range of environmental organisations in her fourth year course, suggested one reason as to why 'it's the only way.'

*'I generally know what's available from personal knowledge. I am aware of certain organisations – it's not anything that comes through the school. We do get sent a lot of leaflets and pamphlets, but then often it doesn't filter down.'*

Some teachers expressed anxieties and reservations about resources being instrumental in the development of curricula.

*'I don't think that any curriculum innovation would have been determined by resources. I know some resources are very attractive. I think we probably look for the concepts and then look for the resources to reinforce those, rather than try to construct a curriculum around resources.'*
(Secondary Deputy Head, Curriculum, Leeds)

*'No, I haven't used any of their (external agencies') stuff. I tend to work from things that I've experienced rather than things I've read about. Because drama is an experiential medium, I often pick up books and read accounts of wonderful drama lessons, but I wouldn't attempt to do that. Whereas if I went to a live session, encountered it, came away thinking, "I can do that, I can handle that experience. . . ." I feel it's very remiss of me to be like that, but that's the way I am.'*
(Secondary Drama Teacher, Leeds)

But a teacher educator, instrumental in launching world studies initiatives in Devon, regards external agency resources as more central to the process of change.

*'Potentially they have a lot of impact. But organisations need to key into developments which are already happening; they need to spend time finding out what is going on in schools, identifying common factors. . . . I actually am a believer that well developed materials can be a catalyst, can induce change. There is no question at all that a lot of teachers are really under pressure to produce interesting curriculum materials of the kind that would sustain course work, and would fit into their GCSE.'*

# Person Power

A second important function of external agencies, from the schools' perspective, is the provision of people who can use their skills and expertise to work with students – either in the classroom or outside school – or with teachers in an in-service capacity. Many reflections on the efficacy of world studies in-service courses – all of which were facilitated by external agencies – can be found in previous chapters. An innovative model of curriculum and professional development, involving staff from the Centre for Global Education working in conjunction with Newcastle Education Authority and Newcastle Polytechnic, is described in the following Case Study.

---

## Case Study 9

## A Partnership for Change

*The following description of an in-service consultancy based in the Walker district of Newcastle upon Tyne is taken from* Co-operating for a Change, *(Newcastle LEA, 1987), a handbook written by the teachers involved in the consultancy. Details of all activities referred to below are to be found in the handbook.*

This is perhaps a unique development in which a comprehensive school (Walker) and its four feeder primary schools (St. Anthony's C of E, Welbeck Road, West Walker and Wharrier Street) are using the world studies philosophy to develop a common approach to learning both within and across phase boundaries. The Head of Lower School at Walker was seconded for the year 1986/7, to co-ordinate the work of twelve teachers – three from each feeder primary school. The primary teachers were seconded for one term so that each term a different teacher from each of the four primary schools was involved. The teachers were all part of a curriculum development workshop established through Newcastle Polytechnic under their long-standing teacher fellowship/workshop programme. The Polytechnic brought in the expertise of a team from the Centre for Global Education (CGE) at York University under consultancy agreements. Ninety per cent of the inset was undertaken by CGE with ten per cent support from the Polytechnic.

As a result of negotiation between the schools, advisers and CGE it was decided that the focus for the three terms' work would be race, gender and the community – the City Council having policy statements covering the first two to which all departments, including education, have to respond and there being a discussion document for the latter. Each term's work was structured in the same way and four stages can be identified:

**Stage 1** – introduction to the philosophy and methodology of world studies;
**Stage 2** – introduction to the focus of the term's work;
**Stage 3** – trialling activities with groups of children in the five schools;
**Stage 4** – evaluation and writing up of the term's work.

The main input at each stage has been from CGE who have run workshops for the group of teachers each term at Walker Lower School. The Polytechnic has supported this work by providing additional resources; enabling each group to share 'good practice' relating to their particular focus within the region by creating links with local educational initiatives; and by identifying strategies to ensure the continued development of the work once all the teachers are back in their own schools.

### Term One: Education for a Multi-Cultural Society in an 'All-White' Urban Context

*Teachers: Tony Baker (Walker School); Denise Baxter (Wharrier Street Junior School); Jim Horrocks (St. Anthony's C of E Primary School); Alan Simpson (West Walker Primary School); George Tiltman (Welbeck Primary School).*

Our focus for the term was multi-cultural and anti-racist education. We read recommended books and articles, studied film and other materials and talked to a number of professionals with interest and expertise in these areas. These, combined with inputs from CGE, succeeded in beginning to raise our awareness of the issues involved. One very important issue to come out of this process was a realisation of how important it is to prepare children in schools like ours, which are virtually all-white, to contribute constructively to life in our multi-cultural society.

In deciding what our approach should be we took a number of things into consideration. We identified a number of characteristics common to the children in the schools where we work and which could form the basis of our activities. We were all aware of the low self-image of many of the children in our area, contributing to lack of motivation and widespread underachievement. We were also aware of the low threshold of tolerance that exists amongst the children and the effect this has upon their ability to get on with one another. Both of these factors, incidentally, are becoming more significant as unemployment and social deprivation increase. We, therefore, realised that an approach to issues of race and culture appropriate to the Walker community needed to start with the enhancement of children's self-esteem and the development of tolerance, co-operation and empathy.

A further concept that we wanted to take into consideration was that of interdependence. We felt that not only are there few opportunities for contact with other cultures, white or black, in Walker, but even amongst children who travel outside the area there is very little awareness of the ways in which individuals and groups in Walker are linked into, and dependent upon, individuals and groups in other places – both in this country and abroad. This was something we thought we could begin to remedy in the activities we planned.

Jim Horrocks developed a programme of activities for 6–7 year olds designed to enhance their self-esteem and then to give them some idea of Newcastle's connections to the wider world. Alan Simpson worked with a class of top infants with the aim of developing self-esteem and co-operation through the themes of helping and being helped, and through the concept of a system. Denise Baxter attempted to use some world studies methods in conjunction with music activity workshops with a class of 9–10 year olds. George Tiltman's principal focus, working with a class of 10–11 year olds, was a cross-cultural simulation game, for which he developed a programme of preparatory activities. Tony Baker's main aim was to introduce the concept of interdependence to a class of 11–12 year olds through a range of activities in preparation for a community project on the local railway line.

City Engineers Photo Unit

*Co-operative Balloons: primary students have to co-operate to get balloons into a basket having only one piece of card each. This activity was devised by Alan Simpson.*

### Term Two: Towards Gender Equality

*Teachers: Tony Baker (Walker School), Angela Fisher (Wharrier Street Junior School); Prue Jackson (Welbeck Primary School); Kathleen Moore (St. Anthony's C of E Primary School); Jean Winterburn (West Walker Primary School).*

At the start of our term's work on gender issues we had varying levels of awareness which we now realise were totally inadequate. As much as fifteen per cent of our time was spent in raising these levels. The following diagram illustrates the awareness-raising process we experienced. This process involved both self-initiated exercises and workshop sessions with the Centre for Global Education.

| | |
|---|---|
| Meeting with Equal Opportunities Teacher Adviser | Introduction to classroom observation schedules, book analysis checklists; sexism in maths books. |
| Viewing of videos on sexism | Changing roles of women; stereotypes; women in science and engineering; history of women's magazines; sexual harassment in schools. |
| Newspaper survey | Images of women and analysis of bias and stereotyping in the popular press. |
| Examples of ongoing work in Newcastle | Meeting and discussion with some local teachers to look at (a) their research on toys and children's literature and (b) examples of 'good practice'. |
| Analysis of 'readers' | Analysis of gender relating to leading roles in a sample of readers in use in schools at the present time. |
| Meeting with Education Librarian | Survey, using checklists, of sexism and racism in a sample of fiction and non-fiction books available from Education Library at Pendower Hall. |
| Workshop sessions with the Centre for Global Education | Introduction to gender issues and gender education. |
| | World studies methodology related to gender issues. |
| Ongoing work in North Tyneside | Presentation at Multi-cultural Centre, Goathland Primary School, by advisory staff on work relating to gender and race in North Tyneside. |

Recognising the importance of co-operation in dealing with gender issues we decided to work co-operatively ourselves and, using world studies techniques, plan a programme of work suitable for children in the four to twelve age range. The programme consisted of four sessions. Each followed a similar pattern: an introductory activity, a main activity and time for children to reflect upon and evaluate what they had been doing. We were conscious of the need to accommodate each child's preferred learning style so we built into each session a period of time when the children could work quietly on their own.

Each session was designed to build on previous work. The first two were specifically designed to foster co-operation and boost self-esteem in preparation for the work on gender awareness covered in the following two sessions. We identified activities which we felt would satisfy the objectives for each session and adapted the apparatus and approach as necessary to suit the varying needs of each group within the four to twelve age range.

Feedback on the activities and sessions was considered to be essential in order to be able to evaluate what we had been doing. Wherever possible, children were encouraged to participate in this process in an enjoyable and non-threatening way. In addition, we kept our own diaries of each session and also collected written and verbal contributions from independent observers. This triangulation method, involving evaluation by children, teachers and other observers, gave us a fairly comprehensive feedback on the effectiveness of activities.

### Term Three: The Just and Fair Community

*Teachers: Tony Baker (Walker School); Marie Davidson (West Walker Primary School); Rosemary Henderson (Wharrier Street School); Pauline Jarvis (Welbeck Primary School); Carol Shields (St. Anthony's C of E School)*

Our way of looking at 'the just and fair community' was through the concept of human rights. There were two reasons for approaching it in this way. First of all we felt that if everyone was granted their basic human rights the community would be much more just and fair. The second reason was that human rights are the unspoken basis for any policy pertaining to fairness and justice and underpin the philosophy relating to race and gender issues upon which the two previous groups had focussed.

As a group our knowledge was limited to the violations of human rights as presented by the media and much publicised by the work of Amnesty International and other organisations. We felt initially that it was a topic having more relevance to some other countries. However, we soon came to realise that problems in our own society such as unemployment, homelessness, poverty and child abuse, are in fact human rights violations.

Parents and governors can be very sympathetic to the idea of human rights education when they are helped to see that the activities involved are based on widely accepted aims of primary education. These aims have always stressed such values as enquiry, tolerance, co-operation, understanding and fairness – essential elements in the teaching of human rights.

The group worked co-operatively. Five sessions were planned, each consisting of an introductory activity, followed by a main activity and a concluding activity. The first two sessions consisted entirely of co-operative activities; the remaining three sessions concentrated upon human rights. The group planned together and trialled the same activities adapting materials supplied by CGE to suit the particular needs of the various age groups and accommodate different learning styles. The same triangulation method of evaluation used by the previous group, involving evaluation by children, teachers and other observers, was used.

**Evaluation**

What we found most useful:

1. The time to reflect. Normal pressures of work make it difficult for teachers to stand back and view objectively what they are doing. The secondment gave us the unique opportunity to reflect on current practice in our own and other schools.

2. World studies methodology. Our introduction to world studies techniques was active and participatory. This gave us a firm foundation on which to evaluate its usefulness. We were immediately convinced of its value in the classroom. All the activities are based within a problem-solving framework and can be adapted for use across the curriculum.

3. Learning styles. Although we were aware that children learn in different ways our understanding was vague. We were introduced to the research work which describes the four preferred modes of learning. This work made us realise the importance of incorporating into each day the chance for every child to learn in their preferred mode. We were shocked to discover that children can be seriously disadvantaged if they are seldom given this opportunity.

4. Strengthening links. The secondment gave us the opportunity to develop personal and professional relationships with colleagues in schools in Walker. The most important development has been the introduction of common approaches to learning in our schools.

Our hopes and expectations in the middle and long term are:

1. We hope for more co-operation within and between schools with joint planning and evaluation among members of staff and more sharing of ideas.

2. We hope to involve our colleagues in world studies through inset.

3. Our long-term aim is to develop a school policy which will add to the ethos of the school and bring world studies methodology into every classroom.

4. We need to make parents, governors and the wider community aware of this work and the ways in which they can be part of its development.

Personnel from outside agencies who come into class can be assessed in terms of their novelty value.

'It's good to have somebody new, somebody different coming in – it makes them listen. You get another slant on it. It was super – it makes you look at things in a different way.'
(Primary Teacher, Newcastle)

In cases where the relationship between agency worker, teacher and students is rather more profound, the impact upon the students' learning is likely to be greater. A Newcastle primary teacher used a development agency worker as a 'team planning adviser and as a physical resource in the classroom' on a project about the Famine in Ireland.

She conjects that the success of such a relationship has 'much to do with personalities. . . . I certainly was very impressed with him as a person, so every time I heard his name or saw him around, I was interested to know what was going on.' A Personal and Social Development team in a North Tyneside secondary school established a similar relationship with a development worker in connection with their Peace and Justice Week.

*'What I think his involvement enabled us to do was to see how we could use participatory learning methods more to address wider issues than the ones we have been used to. It's all very well looking at brushing your teeth or keeping fit; it's an easy thing to do. The contact with OXFAM helped bring in development issues – issues to do with justice. We worked on a global issue and made local links – land rights in Brazil, linked to a motorway going through our community.'*

This teacher also reflects on the significance of the relationship between school and agency worker for bringing about change.

*'I think if it's possible to find space to do that concerted work with teachers – he was in school every lesson for that week, so we got to know each other – that kind of curriculum development can work. So that they (agencies) can be more than peripheral, but it depends on them being able to get into schools . . . the number of packs I've got at home which I've bought and never used – never found the time to go through! The other important element was that the initiative came from the school.'*

With this quotation comes a clear indication of the fallacy of assuming that the publication of new resources is in itself an effective strategy for bringing about change. Set in the context of the realities of a teacher's life, the purchase of a resource pack does not necessarily lead to its utilisation, nor can there by any certainty that the materials will be used in a way which meets the objectives of the designers. This was clearly understood by one development agency.

*'Our emphasis in the future will be on looking at how resources can be used rather than on developing new ones. We shall be hoping to disseminate existing material better, meshing available material with teachers' needs.'*

Where teachers or schools had contact with an environmental agency, the tendency was for the agency worker to take students out of school, to do some local conservation work or explore a burning community issue. A Bradford science teacher considered such contact vital because the students' experience of the natural environment was very limited: 'Some 17 year old girls don't really know what a wood is.' He claimed that the help and expertise of such agencies could make a big difference in that a 'lot of council bureaucracy is involved in practical conservation work.' He suggested, though, that the aims and values of conservation groups were important to establish, as some had an expectation of students 'going out to work for them'.

In a Devon secondary school, where 'the environment' is a strand within the core curriculum, students are encouraged to get personally involved in a local environmental issue and, consequently, to explore the function and utilise the expertise of many external agencies – from conservation groups to planning departments.

*'In fact, last year, some of the students looked at the Dart Port plan. There was a local enquiry at County Hall and they were invited to go along, any of them that were interested were invited to go along by the local Traders' Association. When they got there, they were actually photographed holding a banner – all in school uniform, easily identifiable – but they were the ones holding the banner saying "We want our Dart Port project". They got very involved in it.'*

This aspect of involvement with local agencies and community groups – student empowerment – is considered important by a headteacher in Bradford, in an area 'where things tend to happen to people, they don't influence them – the bus is taken off, the health centre closes. You have to believe that you can make things happen.' One way in which his school hopes to put across that philosophy to students is through the adoption of four detainees in South Africa through Amnesty International. Amnesty has also provided a focus and stimulus for action in the sixth form at a Dorset secondary school, rather exceeding the expectations of the teacher who set it up.

*'I was expecting to get about ten to start an Amnesty group, and in the first session I had over 80. . . . This year we have a group of about 35–40 who are involved mainly in the Urgent Action Scheme, writing for various campaigns, such as the Refugee Campaign. I am getting interest from younger pupils – two fifth formers have joined Amnesty – so the whole thing has started to get going and it has provided a focus for pupils' thinking beyond the UK. We*

*have written to Russia, various African countries, South America, the Far East, really everywhere ... in language lessons pupils have been writing letters in French. We have a lot of members of staff involved, language specialists – Portuguese, Spanish, German, French, Swedish, Italian. What has struck me is that a lot of pupils are very sympath- etic to the problems, they want to know about them and do something, but if I was to go into a classroom and teach that formally I would worry about how much damage I had done – turning people off. By allowing them to be volunteers I feel they have a much greater understanding.'*

For this teacher, the strength of a link with Amnesty Inter- national lay in the legitimation that the organisation could give to practices which some parents might have deemed too controversial.

## Obstacles to change

It is clear from the first part of this chapter that many teachers interviewed had derived much from the resources and services of external agencies. Indeed, it could be argued that without these agencies' support the movement towards holistic education would be much less substantial, given the relatively little encouragement emanating from mainstream sources of curriculum and professional development. External agencies are valiantly filling – albeit partially – a deep lacuna in the provision of support for the growing interest amongst teachers in global and holistic approaches in schools. One question needs to be asked, however: how much *more* effective might these agencies be if they had a clearer understanding of change processes in education? The rest of this chapter will attempt to offer some answers, firstly by exploring some of the major obstacles to change cited by both teachers and agency workers. These fall into three categories: access to school, relationships with schools, and operational difficulties.

A major obstacle that many external agencies face in gaining access to schools is the *perception* of the agency held by teachers, particularly if there is a perceived connection with a charitable or campaigning organisation.

*'Schools are bombarded by outside charities looking for fund-raising. If they approach as another charity, another source to raise money for, then I think they would get a pretty cool reception, because even within this school staff are always saying, "If only we had enough money we could buy this." If they approach schools as providing an*

*educational background to world topics, to life in other countries, then I think they would receive a much more welcoming reception.'*
(Primary Headteacher, Newcastle)

*'I think my only bother about NGOs is always the fund-raising aspect. Schools are bombarded with fund-raising for everything, so I think that very often things tend perhaps to get put in a bin.'*
(Middle School Headteacher, Dorset)

The headteacher cited above claimed that the NGO materials he had seen were 'very good – produced by people who know the inside of a classroom', but he admitted to having dismissed the local development agency as 'another bandwagon' until his deputy had shown that it could offer substantial help with resources. A Newcastle primary teacher also admits to having to overcome her negative preconception of a development agency, after a friend suggested she should go there for resources.

*'I was very loathe to go at first because there is this Christian/colonial type attitude which I immediately think of, I think it's changing, but it still sticks with me, so initially it put a barrier between me going. Now I know what alternative things it can provide which nowhere else caters for. I just override that – but it was a big minus for me.'*

*Percentage of agencies surveyed using the following means of establishing contact with schools/teachers.*

| School/Teacher Contact | % |
| --- | --- |
| through requests from schools/teachers | 71 |
| through requests from students | 29 |
| through direct approach by your staff to schools | 46 |
| through LEA advisors or advisory teachers | 52 |
| through Parent Teacher Associations | 5 |
| through school links of other non-governmental organisations | 27 |

– Global Impact survey of non-governmental organisations and statutory bodies.

Development agency workers are often aware of this problem and feel themselves caught in a trap. Some teachers do expect them to fulfil their 'charitable' functions by coming into school at harvest time to talk about starving children, whilst others want nothing to do with 'Third World charity'. Their position, as two development agency workers expressed it, is further complicated by the unresolved tensions between promoting development education and promoting the image of their parent organisation for the purposes of fund-raising.

Two teachers we interviewed, both influential in developing world studies in their schools, expressed profound dissatisfaction with the 'too pushy and strident approach' adopted by a development agency. One teacher talked of the 'very strained atmosphere' on an after-school in-service course which subsequently closed because the number of participants dwindled; the development worker running the course claimed that 'it was impossible to run sessions outside school hours when directed time came in.' The other teacher commented on a contribution to an in-service weekend.

*'It was the time of Bob Geldof and all she could talk about was how bad he was. I didn't really think he was that bad, and I didn't think she had to be that aggressive about him because nobody on the course actually said that what he was doing was wonderful. Everybody there was reasonably intelligent and thought, "Well, yes, it's alright giving the money, but there should be a little bit more." But she really was quite aggressive – all this giving of money was absolutely appalling, he shouldn't be glorified for that, there should be this, this and this. . . . Several of us said, "There's no reason to talk like that," but she wouldn't have it, she just kept on.'*

This teacher contrasted the aggressive approach of the agency worker with the gradual permeation strategy adopted by his two colleagues on returning from a world studies course: 'Gradually people's perceptions have changed. I think the worst thing they could have done was to try to ram it down somebody's throat. As soon as that happens, they switch off.'

The difficulties for external agencies in gaining access to schools is not helped, it seems, by the nature and quality of the relationship that can exist between the two institutions. In fact, as many interviewees pointed out, the relationship is rarely at an institutional level.

*A man is born gentle and weak.*
*At his death he is hard and stiff.*
*Green plants are tender and filled with sap.*
*At their death they are withered and dry.*

*Therefore the stiff and unbending is the disciple of death.*
*The gentle and yielding is the disciple of life.*

*Thus an army without flexibility never wins a battle.*
*A tree that is unbending is easily broken.*

*The hard and strong will fall.*
*The soft and weak will overcome.*

– Lao Tsu

'*The senior management teams seem to need everything to be legitimised and they question, it seems to me, organisations which are funded by OXFAM or Christian Aid or whatever, as to what their relationship should be with the school. They're quite happy to drag them in for school assembly, and so on . . . but to actually establish a sort of formal relationship between an organisation and a school, it simply doesn't seem to happen.*'
(Secondary Adviser, Dorset)

'*Some NGOs do establish a relationship with the school rather than with the teacher, but I think we come back to the human perception: I've got a nice relationship with a young lady from Help the Aged – it's on a human level, on a personal level, rather than Help the Aged as Help the Aged.*'
(Primary Headteacher, Dorset)

Two development agency workers concurred: 'We tend not to have relationships with schools but with teachers.' They claimed to be rarely contacted by a headteacher or school policy maker and suggested that if they were so contacted, the school would 'doubt our resources.' A Newcastle primary teacher, however, pointed to some reasons for, and strengths in, the person-to-person relationship, based on her own experience.

'*At least you're not concentrating on forging relationships right at the outset, so that you get straight in and do something productive – you've got a project in mind, people you know who are going to work together, but you don't have to spend time messing around finding out how people work, it's very easy. That makes it more efficient.*'

The personal qualities and expertise of the agency worker obviously determine the nature of the relationship with a school, as a theatre-in-education worker pointed out.

*'I think if an outside agency has a teacher working with them with current experience and knowledge of teaching and learning styles, with a commitment to making those more active, that makes a lot of difference. I would hope it's been very helpful for the Company, it's certainly been of great interest to me. I think often outside agencies can be very detached from schools; they want close relationships, but they're not very sure, they haven't got somebody who's an obvious person to liaise.'*

External agencies that tend to work outside the school, as do many conservation groups, are even less likely to have a firm relationship with a school. Such links can be extremely tenuous, with predictable ramifications.

*'The kids either choose to work with us, or in some cases they are sent out, probably problem kids who aren't much good in the classroom, sometimes without a teacher – which I think is wrong. It's not our role to have to discipline them, but we tend to have to.'*
(Environment Worker, West Yorkshire)

A consequence of the person-oriented nature of the relationship between schools and external agencies is that only rarely is the whole school involved in a project or development. The potential for an innovation to be passed on from one teacher to another is limited by the usual constraints of lack of time and poor internal communication, particularly where the headteacher or senior management team are not involved in, or are largely ignorant of the innovation. One development worker, whilst accepting that the whole school is the 'logical target', was wary about the whole school approach, in that 'you need a carefully defined contract and need to be confident of the support of the whole staff – otherwise you can find yourself dealing with intransigents, people who think things are a communist plot!' The absence of a negotiated, considered relationship is likely to limit, too, the prospects for continuity, follow-up work and evaluation. Whilst many agencies resist teachers' pleas for 'one-off' talks, slide-shows or performances – unless there is a good chance of subsequent involvement at a deeper level – they regard themselves very much as 'pump-primers' or initiators of a change process. In some cases this is a reflection of the agency's policy, as implied by one conservation worker: 'Schools will get the newsletter, with ideas on maintenance. If it goes well, we

> *I have no commitment to change as a panacea. In fact the real goal is continuity, which is a kind of stability. The splendid evolutionary paradox is that continuity requires constant sensitive readjustment – not only change but precise change.*
> – Stewart Brand

don't hear from them.' In others, it is simply a result of limited personnel and resources, being expected to cover a large number of schools over a wide geographical area: 'Each school is limited to a maximum of one term, partly to involve more schools and also so they don't get bored.' (Environment Worker, West Yorkshire)

*Percentage of agencies surveyed claiming the following types of link with schools/teachers.*

| School/Teacher Links | % |
| --- | --- |
| one-off project/visit with an individual school (including visiting speakers) | 54 |
| on-going projects with schools/groups of schools | 50 |
| involvement in initial teacher training | 22 |
| involvement in in-service teacher training | 43 |
| the mounting of shows/exhibitions visited by schools | 36 |
| educational conferences for teachers/students | 33 |
| running teachers' resources centre | 14 |
| running resources information service used by teachers | 34 |

– Global Impact survey of non-governmental organisations and statutory bodies.

As we have seen, contact between schools and external agencies may be restricted for a number of reasons. Some of these can be ascribed to the operational difficulties under which agencies constantly work. In any catalogue of operational constraints compiled by external agencies, funding will almost certainly be near the top. Many smaller agencies rely on income from charitable sources which is both limited in quantity and uncertain in continuance. Those which attract governmental finance – through MSC schemes, for example – are seemingly not much better off. One environmental agency talked of 'the uncertain future of MSC funding' and the need to approach charitable trusts and industry, whilst another cited the 'pressure of impressing MSC with the quality of our work – having to justify our exist-

> *With a school that hasn't any contact with us before, we would take on just running an assembly, which I don't see as an exercise in development education for the children at all, but might be just the very first stage to some sort of credibility for us in school, which we can then build on. But if we took an assembly in a school now, for twenty minutes, sometimes perhaps ten, I think we certainly wouldn't do that a second time, they've got to commit themselves a bit more the second time, so that it's just the beginning of a sort of growth.*
>
> – Development Worker

ence every month' as a real constraint. An uncertain future causes many problems in staff recruitment.

*'The team changes every year. We never know if a scheme is going to survive next month – there's a permanent threat of closure. It can be difficult to get good staff: at Field Officer level we lose a lot of credibility with the local authority because people are always changing.'*
(Schools Co-ordinator, an Environment Agency, West Yorkshire)

Linked to staffing difficulties is an agency's capacity to publicise their resources and services and, subsequently, to meet the demand they might create. Many agencies rely solely on 'word of mouth' publicity, though use of LEA mailing systems was mentioned where there were good links with the advisory service. The existence of external agencies is therefore unknown to very many teachers.

*'I think a lot of people don't know that (the centre) exists. I didn't until last year, somebody . . . it was word of mouth. It was quite an eye-opener to find it: to find some of the stuff that was in there.'*
(Primary Teacher, Newcastle)

The real problem, according to one development worker, is that he wanted more people to be interested in what the agency had to offer but he realised that they could not cope with an increased demand at present levels of funding and staffing. One environmental agency in West Yorkshire, however, has had to change its policy over publicity.

*'We've possibly slit our own throats by not advertising. People at the top of education, in the Nature Conservancy Council and so on, didn't know this work was happening because we go in at a level that gets the work done, but don't feed anything upwards. Now we're shouting from the*

*rooftops and producing a report on work since 1980. We
need to do this to survive.'*

The uneasy balance between promotion and 'getting work
done', between satisfying the needs of teachers and meeting
the demands of present or potential sponsors, is one with
which most external agencies have to contend. It is even
more difficult in a political climate which, in the view of
one development worker, is 'totally antipathetic to our
kind of work'. In this regard, environmental agencies –
particularly those which focus on conservation – are at less
of a disadvantage. 'Nature areas generally seem to be "in",
everybody wants one and there's lots of resources and
support available. This kind of work will always have a
future.'

A further constraint, expressed by many agency workers,
arises from the relative inflexibility of school timetables and
examination syllabus requirements, exacerbated by some
equally rigid thinking on the part of teachers. This problem
is obviously far worse in secondary schools.

*'I think really, working in high schools is very hard because
of the exams, because of the pressure of time, the "I've got
my syllabus to get through, I haven't got time, we're not
going to start looking at what happened in India a long
time ago, we're not doing that this year." If the kids are
looking at what happened in India at the time of independence with their history teachers, that's OK, but if they then
want to examine the morality, the strains on relationships –
all things that should come out of the play called "Raj" –
they don't feel it should be happening in their time. It's
difficult to convince people that the skills are transferable,
that we want kids to question what's put in front of them,
to see the truth, to look for their own opinions; and that all
the looking and reading and finding out is producing actual,
real concrete skills which are well-used in future history
lessons. So it's making people see that there is a very real
value, and it's worth being flexible with the timetable.'*
(Theatre-in-Education Worker, West Yorkshire)

Environmental organisations tended to have more contact
with primary and middle schools, where the response from
students to such activities as practical conservation work,
nature walks and pond dipping is 'fantastic . . . they love
it. But by the secondary age a lot of that has gone.'

# Change from without . . . or without change?

Drawing on the evidence so far presented in this chapter, there can be no doubt that the task of external agencies, that of promoting change from outside the school system, is complex, frustrating and time-consuming. That much is certainly not news, being an integral part of the daily experience of most agency workers. Yet, despite the considerable obstacles, there is also ample evidence throughout this book of considerable success: of agencies throwing out life-lines to disillusioned teachers; of agency resources and personnel being highly valued. Can this be attributed to sheer chance, to the happy coincidence of teacher need and agency service occurring at the same time and place? Our thesis, expounded in the exploration of change processes outlined in Chapter Two, refutes this suggestion. Where real change has taken place, it has occurred because the individuals and organisations involved have demonstrated an understanding of change as a multi-dimensional process and have appreciated the need for personal meaning. If external agencies working for change towards holistic education are to have more impact on teachers and schools in the future they must acquire more knowledge of and sensitivity to the change process. For, beyond the success stories lie countless examples of minimal or non-change. This is due, we contend, to the pervasive influence of unholistic thinking and practice – not in all external agencies, or at least, not in all aspects of their operation, but in enough to warrant a fundamental review of philosophy and practice. Never before in the history of education have there been so many potential sources of positive influence from outside the system: organisations, groups and individuals who can take a broader view; who can spend time developing resources and expertise which more accurately reflect and respond to a systemic, holistic worldview. Never before . . . and, perhaps, if the opportunity is not seized and the fragmentationalist tendencies of current educational reforms take hold, never again – or at least not in time to save the next few generations of students from a limited and limiting school experience. Whilst acknowledging, as members of an external agency ourselves, the difficulties of operating holistically, we offer in all humility, the following guidelines.

*We have gone to the Moon but do not know yet how to make a flame tree or a birdsong. Let us keep our dear countries free from irreversible mistakes which would lead us in the future to long for those same birds and trees.*

– President Houphouet-Boigny
of the Ivory Coast

## 1. Beware of polarisation

At a recent conference on the future of global education,[3] the development education workers present issued a strong, unified statement: 'The value system of development education is fundamentally opposed to the value system of the current (political) regime.' Being in opposition in the present climate, it was felt, was threatening the agencies' fund-raising potential and their charitable status. Thus it was necessary, some argued, 'To stand firm – resist', 'To act as a government in exile,' to continue to support teachers, schools and LEAs – 'They're not afraid of us.' Whilst the message of continued support is heartening, perhaps some lessons might be learnt from the history of political impotance enjoyed by so many governments in exile. We have evidence, some cited in this book, of teachers, schools and LEAs who are indeed 'afraid' – not of the sensitive, innovatory and exciting resources and services offered by many external agencies, but of the overt campaigning, the polemics and the 'right answers' peddled by some. Polarisation induces retrenchment, not change.

---

*Touching every area of our lives, there is an Invisible Planet, rarely seen on television or read about in newspapers. It is a state of ideas and visions and practical enterprises that people move in and out of depending on their moods and needs, a domain that is very new, and at the same time, very old.*

*Networks are the meeting grounds for the inhabitants of this invisible domain. These flexible, vibrant organizations often exist without boundaries, bylaws, or officers. Networks are the lines of communication, the alternative express highways that people use to get things done. In crisis and in opportunity, the word spreads quickly through these people-power lines.*

*– Jessica Lipnack & Jeffrey Stamps*

---

## 2. Beware of isolation

The essence of holistic change is connectedness. Amongst external agencies can be detected narrow visions of connectedness, tram-line alignments of organisations with similar ideologies and educational interests calling themselves 'networks'. Let us remind ourselves that genuine networking, according to Virginia Hine, 'encourages full utilisation of individual and small group innovation . . . promotes maximum penetration of ideas across socio-economic and cultural barriers while preserving cultural and subcultural diversity . . . and puts a structural premium on egalitarian and personalistic skills.'[4] Let us remind ourselves, too, whether we 'belong' to an environment, development or other agency, that ours is not the only organisation working for a more holistic, humane education; nor will we achieve that goal alone. As well as national and international conferences of like-minds, there is an urgent need for local liaisons with community and youth groups, with parents and governors, with people who share, perhaps, different perspectives and priorities. Their involvement is necessary to the change process. The call for 'unification', often heard amongst scattered organisations professing similar beliefs, is understandable in a system where power is achieved through fragmentation and protectionism. The centralised power of an isolated empire is a lot easier to smash, however, than are the subtle influences of a pervasive network.

### 3. Beware of fragmentation

'As an organisation, we follow the famous quotation, "think globally, act locally" – we're the "act locally". That's what we're good at, we don't see any reason why we should change that. There are other organisations around that cover the global side.' A classic example, from an environment worker, of 'un-global' thinking, echoed by very many environmental agencies in their fragmented approach to the school curriculum, in which they 'stressed basic ecological principles and endangered species whilst eschewing the social, economical and political aspects.'[5] Fragmentation is evident too in the failure of many agencies to adopt a whole-school approach: whilst a personal relationship with an individual teacher may be productive at one level, it needs to be recognised that she is part of a wider system. New opportunities for whole-school development are presenting themselves. 'The "Baker Days" are in fact a boon to us', admitted one development worker, 'though we keep fairly quiet about it because it's not too popular a thing to say.' Concealed within these arcane possibilities for gaining access into schools is the temptation to practise the 'hit and run model' of professional development: the one-off blockbuster which shatters assumptions and illusions and promises no further support for those who need re-building. Lack of follow-up and evaluation – admitted by many external agencies – is another indication of a misunderstanding of the change process, as is an over-emphasis on the production of classroom resources. Agencies which obtain funding for resource production, but little or no money for dissemination and education in the *use* of those resources, are operating to as similarly a limited view of change as evinced by the curriculum development projects of the 1960s. Their prospects for inducing long-term change are certainly no better.

### 4. Beware of Messianic zeal

'There is a desperate need for change on every level – local, national, global – in order to survive in a way that is humane and fair. The world is a very disharmonious place.' Possibly few reading this book would disagree with this development worker's analysis of the state of the planet. But just as Bob Geldof did not have all the answers, neither do we – we are merely part of a dynamic process. The campaigning approach – the extremist path which claims the truth as its own – is neither educational nor conducive to change for it denies to the individual any stake in the process. It also denies that any one else can be working for change – 'You've got so much apathy, haven't you?' said one environment worker about attitudes to the environment. Messianic zeal does not replace apathy with involvement, but with fundamentalist dependence.

### 5. Beware of confusion

*It is favourable to have some goal in view.*
*– I Ching, 28 & 32*

A 'lack of clarity over aims' was a common admission amongst external agencies. 'I don't think anybody has ever set down an actual goal. To be honest, I would doubt the educational value of a lot of the work that we do. . . . I don't think you learn much from painting railings, clearing mud off a path or dredging a pond – you certainly don't learn anything doing it a second time.' This sorry admission from an environment worker reveals not only confusion over aims but also a limited conception of education. Without a clear set of aims, based upon a sound grasp of the diverse ways in which students and teachers learn, the contribution of external agencies towards change will be minimal. Without establishing our aims, evaluation becomes impossible; without evaluation, we shall never know if we make any impact at all.

# References

1. See Greig, S., Pike, G. & Selby, D., *Global Impact: First Year Report*, Centre for Global Education, 1987, 46–75.

2. A series of seven booklets produced by the Development Education Project, Manchester, published in 1985.

3. 'Education for Global Futures', a conference for teachers, educationists and external agency workers, held at Losehill Hall, Derbyshire, 11–13 March 1988, as part of the Global Impact Project (see Chapter Three, reference 1).

4. Hine, V. H., 'The basic paradigm of a future socio-cultural system', *World Issues*, April/May 1977, 19, cited in Elgin, D., *Voluntary Simplicity*, William Morrow, 1981, 292.

5. Greig, S., *et al.*, *op. cit.*, 68.

### In Time of 'The Breaking of Nations'

Only a man harrowing clods
In a slow silent walk
With an old horse that stumbles and nods
Half asleep as they stalk.

Only thin smoke without flame
From the heaps of couch-grass;
Yet this will go onward the same
Though Dynasties pass.

Yonder a maid and her wight
Come whispering by:
War's annals will cloud into night
Ere their story die.

– Thomas Hardy

·CHAPTER SEVEN·

# The National Curriculum: Crisis or Opportunity?

*'The national curriculum is a worry, clearly; possible scenarios vary from the very pessimistic to the optimistic.'*
(Secondary Head of Department, Devon)

As our research was carried out during a period of mounting speculation, but little hard evidence, concerning the shape and force of a national curriculum it is not surprising that teachers' reactions to its introduction should vary; nor is it difficult to understand why their responses were commonly tempered with caution and anxiety. Our research, after all, took place during a time in which the most radical transformation of the education system for forty-five years was being formulated, and yet the basic assumptions, ideals and goals of this innovation remained a mystery to the vast majority of the teaching profession, whose only source of clues were the enigmatic – and often contradictory – statements of ministers.

Our intention in this chapter is not to debate what should or should not be in a national curriculum which is appropriate for education in the late twentieth century; that has been – and continues to be – cogently and passionately debated in many other places. Our starting point is the certainty that a national curriculum, in some shape or form, will have to be addressed by all primary and secondary teachers as one of their principal professional responsibilities. What are the chances of the proposals being faithfully and successfully implemented? Given all that we have learnt about the problems associated with educational innovation over the last thirty years, what is the likely impact of this reform on the lives of teachers, on whom its ultimate success or failure depends? Are we engaged, as many teachers have expressed, in a deepening crisis in education, or is it a time of unparalleled opportunity? According to ancient Chinese wisdom, the two positions are connected, not contradictory: one's perception of the task ahead provides a key.

# Crisis

*'With the changes, we will possibly have to re-prioritise because it's not a matter of what you want to do but of what you have to do for 90% of the time.'*
(Junior School Headteacher, Newcastle)

*'I see world studies and what it stands for as under threat and assault from present educational reforms. The teachers' own view of how the national curriculum will work and what will actually happen in schools, is still at a relatively crude stage, so they see the national curriculum in terms of enormous blocks of time that have to be done for this, this, this and this, and in terms of the simple question of squeezing out. And there's a political dimension to this, too; it has become less respectable. You can see this happening in all sorts of areas to do with homosexuality and things like that. Heads will be looking at their governing bodies, who are bound to become much more important – even more important than they are now – before they have controversial issues tackled within their school because they'll be thinking "Well, who's going to haul me over the coals over this one?"'*
(Secondary Adviser)

*'One constraint clearly is the national curriculum – history, geography – it appeals to the reactionary instincts of people who can recognise something. It's back to the "sabre-toothed curriculum". There is a huge flaw in this – it doesn't work unless you've got economic and social stability and those things will not guarantee you that.'*
(Secondary Headteacher, Devon)

From our understanding of educational change as discussed in Chapter Two, it has to be said that the prospects for teachers and for schools during the initial implementation phase of the national curriculum are not rosy. The proposals emanating from the DES have seemingly failed to take account of two crucial aspects of innovation in education: the need for teachers to find personal meaning in any proposed change, and an appreciation of the culture of the school. The 'gap between worlds', the gulf in ideals and experience between the educationist reformer and the classroom practitioner, which marred so many previous attempts at curriculum change, is in this instance a yawning chasm. Not only are there customary differences in the perception of schooling between many classroom teachers and those who have been selected to shape the national curriculum in their subject working groups, but there exists a further divide – it has emerged – between this latter group and the DES, not to mention the schisms within the Cabinet itself. We thus have the farcical situation of a national curriculum, a major shift in educational policy, seemingly not determined by a thoroughgoing analysis of educational needs, nor guided by the collective wisdom of the teaching profession, but founded on the values and beliefs of public servants and politicians, many of whose vision of education we can only guess at.

Some teachers, by coincidence, clearly agree with the basic concept of a national curriculum, a guiding framework to standardise educational provision throughout England and Wales. (Some of the underlying values are implicit, of course, in the very title of 'national' curriculum: whose nation is being referred to?) But what opportunities are open even to them to claim a stake in this innovation, to find meaning? There is scant recognition of change as a personal learning process in the timetable of imple-mentation laid down. The haste with which this major reform is being inscribed in the statute book owes little to immediate educational necessities (unlike the post-Sputnik innovations) and shows alarming blindness to the needs of a profession already demoralised and understaffed. The meagre provision of financial assistance to provide essential in-service training and support all adds to the impression of political expediency and engineering masquerading under the guise of educational reform. Just as the national curriculum proposals themselves show ignorance of the importance of teaching and learning styles, so the imple-mentation plans have little concern for the various learning needs of teachers.

If one applies the 'practicality ethic' (see page 43), as many teachers are no doubt doing, prospects for the successful implementation of the national curriculum look slim indeed. In the first place, the *need* is unclear; many teachers would agree that there are a range of problems in edu-cational provision, but there would be some doubt as to which problems, if any, the national curriculum addresses.

*'Now, we do not have clarity of purpose about education, but I see the national curriculum as one of the most reaction-ary statements about education ever made. We're pro an*

*entitlement curriculum, but it should be based on a rigorous analysis of the outputs of education – and you can't distinguish the outputs from the means – which is why the developments in this school are so important.'*
(Secondary Headteacher, Devon)

For the pessimist, the national curriculum is likely to create more needs than it satisfies – a recipe for disaster in terms of the destiny of an innovation. Secondly, considerable confusion and anxiety exists, and will doubtless persist, over the day-to-day tasks of the teacher in fulfilling the requirements of the national curriculum. How much more time and energy will it consume? What new skills will have to be learnt? How will it affect existing priorities and sense of job satisfaction? A provisional assessment of such questions suggests, for many teachers, that the rewards are likely to be far outweighed by the costs.

As we have shown in earlier chapters, the success of any educational innovation is largely dependent upon the degree of receptiveness and ownership on the part of the teacher. The national curriculum proposals have attempted to overcome this major stumbling block of previous grand designs for schooling through simply brandishing the weapon of coercion. Unlike most curriculum reforms of the past thirty years, the national curriculum is mandatory, not only supported by legislation but also powerfully assisted by new schemes for student assessment and teacher appraisal. Is this innovation likely to succeed, then, despite ignoring the lessons of history? Judgement of success, of course, is subjective, particularly when the goals are not clearly identified in the first place. Michael Fullan provides a clue in his analysis of change as requiring a combination of *pressure* and *support*.[1] Clearly, in terms of the proposed national curriculum, there is an abundance of the former and a dearth of the latter. A likely result of this imbalance is one particular form of non-change, identified by Fullan as 'painful unclarity', 'experienced when unclear innovations are attempted under conditions which do not support the development of the subjective meaning of change.'[2] Another likely outcome is an increase in levels of anxiety, stress and dissatisfaction as teachers grapple, amidst mounting pressure, to carry out an innovation in which they have no sense of ownership or control.

# Opportunity

Some interviewees felt that the changes that had already taken root in their schools would be little affected by the imposition of the national curriculum.

*An alternative GERBIL*

G   *Girl friendly and generous and greening,*
E   *Equality, focussed and empowering,*
R   *Racial justice, raising and renewing,*
B   *Beauty begetting and birthing,*
I   *Identity, strengthening and illuming,*
L   *Life, love centred and liberating.*

– Robin Richardson

*'The challenge of the national curriculum? I don't fear that at all. We have our own curriculum; it is the national curriculum; the question is how it's delivered. I think all the approaches we've developed – global education, multi-cultural education and so on – will continue. The challenge is the increasing management of our own affairs which I welcome. They said of TVEI it will restrain the curriculum, impose this and that, we've used it to expand what we are doing. I'm not too afraid of the future.'*
(Secondary Headteacher, Newcastle)

*'Our 75% core is important (maths, english, science, world studies, PE, social education, creative studies, languages – all do a modern language for five years). The national curriculum? We are doing it! Next academic year possibly, we'll take away more periods from extension subjects and increase the core – aiming over two years to have 100% core and probably a more modular curriculum. This is one way of ensuring the present liberal-type curriculum and yet meeting the demands of the national curriculum.'*
(Secondary Deputy Headteacher, Curriculum, Devon)

*'We're optimists. It doesn't matter in a way what central government does because* they don't do it. *Teachers need to be an examplar of how a mature, stable adult conducts their life, often in unreasonable circumstances. If we can do that irrespective of what gets thrust on us and demonstrate how to respond to things which are none of our choosing, then we're providing the best possible education.'*
(Secondary Headteacher, Devon)

Others saw the national curriculum as providing the opportunity for the development of a more holistic curriculum in schools that had remained married to a fossilised, traditional model. The 'Heineken principle' would come into operation allowing change to reach parts it had failed to reach before.

*'Once the national curriculum starts to get in place, my own feeling is that it's going to raise some issues that perhaps not*

*all schools have thought of yet, like how do you manage
cross-curricular delivery of certain themes. There's perhaps
this kind of perceived structural block at the moment, and
it may turn out to be a little bit different in reality.'*
(Secondary Adviser)

*'I may surprise myself saying this but I actually think the
national curriculum is going to help us here. I wouldn't say
it was going to help necessarily in other parts of the country
but it's going to help us because we have so many schools
still committed to a very, very old-fashioned open cafeteria-
type option scheme, and I think there are so many crucial
areas of experience which our kids miss out on, but they
cannot carry on any longer like that because of the national
curriculum, and because of TVEI extension. Those two
things together are a heaven-sent opportunity to get all the
world studies issues – environmental education, political
education, multi-cultural education – onto the agenda. The
national curriculum at this moment in time is a big help
because we have a situation where people do conform. If
something comes from on high, there's that conformist
nature in so many of our people that legitimises things in a
way which can be of enormous help to us.'*
(Senior Adviser, Secondary Education)

*'I'm optimistic that in fact the national curriculum – whilst
at the moment it appears likely to consolidate the old structures and power bases – it could just cause some upheaval
and sufficient instability for opportunities, again using it in
an approving way, to develop things. And that's where I
think that the kind of area that you're interested in, the
links between environmental and development education,
that might present opportunities for that.'*
(University Lecturer in Education)

The tentatively positive note struck by the many interviewees accords well with the multi-faceted view of change
put forward in this book. The national curriculum is a huge
undertaking. Its very magnitude makes it entirely uncertain
how decisions reached in Westminster will ultimately turn
out when they reach the microcosm of the classroom.
Every twist and turn of the decision-making and implementation process, from the subject working group to the
particular in-school departmental meeting, is likely to
divert, in myriad subtle ways, the early intentions of the
originators (their intentions will shift as the process
unfolds). As the last quotation given above indicates, there
will be change agents in abundance at every level looking
for opportunities to use the envisaged reform to their
advantage. As Michael Fullan, drawing upon Peter Rucker,

has pointed out, 'effective entrepreneurs exploit innovation.'[3] In a development as vast as the national curriculum, the entrepreneur is faced with an embarrassment of riches. For proponents of global/holistic education where do some of the best opportunities for influencing the change process triggered by Kenneth Baker lie?

In the first place, they can point to statements made in the original *National Curriculum Consultation Document* of July 1987 and to government interpretations of the Education Reform Bill of 1988 during its passage through Parliament as legitimising a global perspective in the curriculum. The *Consultation Document* called for 'a school curriculum which will develop the potential of all pupils and equip them for the responsibilities for citizenship and for the challenges of employment in tomorrow's world.'[4] It argued that standards of attainment will be raised by 'ensuring that all pupils study a broad and balanced range of subjects throughout their compulsory schooling . . . which will help to develop their capacity to adapt and respond flexibly to a changing world.'[5] Subject working groups, we were informed, would be expected to ensure that 'programmes of work contribute to the development in young people of personal qualities and competence, such as self-reliance, self-discipline, an enterprising approach and the ability to solve practical real-world problems.'[6] In the debate on the Reform Bill in the House of Lords on 21 June 1988, Lord Arran, for the government, argued that the statement in Clause 1 of the Bill that the school curriculum should promote 'the spiritual, moral, cultural, mental and physical development of pupils at the school and of society,' and prepare pupils for 'the opportunities, responsibilities and experiences of adult life' adequately covered the need for a global perspective in schools. 'To understand fully one's own community,' Lord Arran said, 'one must be aware of that wider context and of the complex inter-relationships that knot together all humanity. An awareness of global concerns, those that affect all pupils as "inhabitants of the earth" is thus implied automatically in our reference to "society".' The existing wording of the Bill thus covered 'the concommitant need to understand the world and the complex inter-relationships on which our existence depends.'[7]

In the second place, those responsible for drawing up the national curriculum have wisely left the door open for schools to continue with or adopt interdisciplinary approaches to curricular delivery. The *Consultation Document* made clear that 'the description of the national curriculum in terms of foundation subjects is not a description of how the school day should be organised and the curriculum delivered.'[8] In his major speech at Manchester not long after details of the national curriculum had been released, Kenneth Baker elaborated on this point. 'Perhaps what our critics are saying is, not that the core subjects are out of date, but that schools should not organise their timetables by subjects. I shall not be telling schools how to organise the school day. It is the end-result that matters, not the means of getting there. The pupils must in the end know history, understand science and be able to write English and solve mathematical problems. They may get there by project work or integrated studies. Integrated studies are, I recognise, of particular importance for primary schools. Let me say clearly that we are not trying to suppress project work or eliminate themes. I do – I assure you – understand the importance of teaching traditional subjects across the curriculum in varied and imaginative ways.'[9] The further development of interdisciplinary core or modular courses, emphasising the connectedness between different areas of human experience and endeavour and between the development of human societies and the natural environment, is thus entirely possible under the umbrella of the national curriculum. The opportunity is there for change agents to exploit. Indeed, if one takes into account the demands of GCSE and TVEI extension for 14–16 year old students, modular or integrated courses provide the only way, short of extending the school day, of effectively teaching a curriculum which has been estimated at comprising 120 per cent of the timetable.[10]

It may well be, as some of the teachers and educationalists quoted earlier suggest, that the pressure on schools to develop a more holistic curriculum will actually become greater under the national curriculum. The *Consultation Document* dealt somewhat fleetingly with the proposal that an unspecified number of cross-curricular themes should be 'taught through other subjects'. Disappointingly, the only examples given were health education and use of information technology.[11] In his September 1987 Manchester speech, Kenneth Baker expanded the list. 'I am told we should have included careers education, environmental education, economic awareness, safety, information technology skills, and so on. In fact there is reference to these types of topics: we expect them to be taught through other subjects, giving added dimension to what is taught, as most of them are now in the most effective schools.'[12] In May 1988 one of the present authors wrote to the Department of Education and Science asking for clarification of the place of human rights within the national curriculum given that the government was a signatory to the Council of

Europe's Recommendation R(85)7 on teaching and learning about human rights in schools. The reply explained that the working groups already established had 'been asked to have particular regard to the development of general personal qualities in young people, including a sense of social responsibility. Other working groups will receive a similar remit. The working groups are also being asked to pay special attention to cross-curricular themes and issues which touch upon several different subjects: education about human rights will no doubt be among those.'[13] Letters in a similar vein have been received by environmental education groups with regard to the place of environmental education across the curriculum. It is clear that cross-curricular themes have assumed greater importance since the publication of the *Consultation Document* in June 1987 and, as the Secretary of State acts upon the reports of subject working groups, we may well see schools and departments that have previously shown little inclination to pick up global themes having to take them on board. The auguries are good if we take the *Science for ages 5 to 16* proposals as the standard (the document offers rich opportunities for a more holistic, cross-curricular approach to science embracing the treatment of values); they are less immediately auspicious if we examine its mathematics counterpart.[14]

Fourthly, the national curriculum has adopted a *laissez-faire* approach to matters of classroom process. Scope for the diversity of teaching and learning styles, so central to whole person, whole planet education, remains as before. As the *Consultation Document* puts it: 'How teaching is organised and the teaching approaches used will be for schools to determine. . . . There must be space to accommodate the enterprise of teachers, offering them sufficient flexibility in the choice of content to adapt what they teach to the needs of the individual pupils, to try out and develop new approaches, and to develop in pupils those personal qualities which cannot be written into a programme of study or attainment target.'[15] In this book we have presented a great deal of evidence illustrating the impact of co-operative participatory learning styles on teachers and students alike. A number of teachers and advisers interviewed admitted to being first drawn to the learning activities and, only subsequently, to the accompanying themes and issues. The promotion of interactive learning by inservice educators and agencies alike is, perhaps, the most potent means available for influencing the national curriculum in an holistic direction.

An early, small yet significant instance of how groups and individuals involved in global education can latch on to and exploit changes introduced under the national curriculum has been provided by the Centre for Development Education, Carmarthen. In the autumn of 1988, the Centre published a new 8–13 teaching pack on the Arctic environment, *An Arctic Child*. Written, piloted and published before the national curriculum science working group reported, the pack was marketed as offering an attractive means of meeting most of the objectives laid down by the group. 'Quite fortuitously, it covers 13 of the 17 attainment targets identified in the science document and meets the attainment levels 3–5 (ages 7–11).' The promotional material also announced a two-day residential course on the pack to 'include practical sessions on how the pack meets the demands of the National Curriculum for Science.'[16]

The Centre for Global Education at the University of York has been commissioned by the World Wide Fund for Nature to undertake a three-year project, in partnership with groups of teachers, aimed at developing and disseminating units and activities that add a global dimension to the programme of study laid down under the national curriculum. The project, beginning in September 1989, will cover all the foundation subjects as well as exploring interdisciplinary strategies for meeting the single subject objectives. The project represents a major initiative directed at dovetailing holistic education with the new educational landscape of the 1990s.

In highlighting some of the opportunities it appears are offered by the national curriculum, our intention is not to ignore or minimise the reactionary impulse that lay behind its formulation or the regressive nature of some of its elements. The 'United Kingdom Limited' utilitarian tone of much of the *Consultation Document* and of much that has been said by ministers should alert us to the many potential dangers the education system faces – dangers such as the ossification of the curriculum through the very process of naming subjects as statutory requirements; such as the sense of legitimation felt by traditionalist teachers for maintaining established and outmoded practices in the classroom; such as the straightjacketing of teacher innovation as schools focus narrowly on the needs of assessment at 7, 11, 14 and 16; such as the prospect of 'cross-curricular themes' going the way of 'Language across the Curriculum' and being lost as no particular teacher's priority or responsibility.

We prefer to see the recent educational reform package as a significant landmark in the process of challenge and counter challenge that marks the decline of the old paradigm in the face of the new. Already there are growing rumbles of dissatisfaction amongst disciples of the 'new Right' about the way educational reform is turning out in practice. Having anticipated a vigorous, sustained and wholesale challenge to 'progressivism' in education, their frustration is beginning to show as some of their most cherished articles of reform fail to materialise in the way they had expected.[17] It is up to the teachers and educationalists described in this book, and thousands more like them, to cultivate what is beneficial in the national curriculum whilst actively seeking to reverse or redirect those manifestations of reaction it undoubtedly contains. If the current counter-challenge can be successfully exploited by the 'conspirators', the final wholesale breakthrough of an holistic paradigm for education may not be too far distant.

# References

1. Michael Fullan speaking at the National Foundation for Educational Research, Slough, 11 May 1987.

2. Fullan, M., *The Meaning of Educational Change*, New York, Teachers College Press, 1982, 28.

3. Michael Fullan speaking at the National Foundation for Educational Research, Slough, 11 May 1987.

4. Department of Education and Science Welsh Office, *The National Curriculum 5–16. A Consultation Document*, July 1987, 2, para. 4.

5. *Ibid.*, 3, para. 8(1).

6. *Ibid.*, 25, para. 68.

7. Cited in *Education Reform Bill: Note on report stage in House of Lords*, NADEC, September 1988, 2.

8. Department of Education and Science Welsh Office, *op. cit.*, 9, para. 22.

9. *The Times Educational Supplement*, 25.9.1987, 15, col. 2.

10. See Peter Cornall's 'Model timetable for the 1990s', in *The Guardian*, 31.1.1989, 23, cols. 5–8.

11. Department of Education and Science Welsh Office, *op. cit.*, 8, para. 18.

12. *The Times Educational Supplement*, 25.9.1987, 15, cols. 3–4.

13. A. R. Lin to Selby, June 1988, ref. SX12/169/0165.

14. Department of Education and Science Welsh Office, *Science for ages 5 to 16*, August 1988; Department of Education and Science Welsh Office, Mathematics for Ages 5 to 16; 1988.

15. Department of Education and Science Welsh Office, *The National Curriculum 5–16*. A Consultation Document, July 1987, 11, para. 27.

16. Centre for Development Education, *National Curriculum – Science* (promotional flier), Carmarthen, 1988.

17. See, for instance, Stuart Sexton's article, 'An outside bet to beat 7-year hitch' in *The Guardian*, 3.1.1989, 17. Sexton complains of the Schools Examinations and Assessment Council's decision to offer contracts to three progressive educational groups to develop the attainment targets and assessment procedures required for 7-year-olds under the national curriculum. 'Those of us who suggested some form of understandable, simple, nationwide assessment had in mind an assessment of the child's achievement in the 3Rs or to use today's jargon, in literacy and numeracy. . . . The contracts, however, seem to suggest quite a different approach. It would seem that the assessments of 7-year-olds are not going to check literacy and numeracy, but rather to specify certain arbitrarily chosen methods of teaching, and then to test the results of those methods. Further, the assessment is apparently to be by the child's own teachers.'

# Greenprints for Changing Schools

**A: Understanding change processes**

1. Change is an organic process, a natural result of the dynamic interaction between all parts of a system. If change does not occur it is evidence of blockages within the system which need to be dislodged or dissolved. Change itself changes: it evolves constantly as influenced by people and institutions. Change is provisional and never-ending, a process out of which there is no final product.

2. Change is multi-faceted. It can be triggered – or blocked – by any part, at any level, of a system. It has inner and outer dimensions, requiring personal and institutional commitment. The force and direction of change is unpredictable, but its impact can be maximised by seeking to connect 'conspirators', linking diverse 'islands' of change so as to create a new 'landmass'. Networking is the most appropriate form of organisation to promote and sustain change.

3. Change requires clarity of purpose. A shared set of values amongst all those involved in change will facilitate its progress. A clear statement of aims, understood and agreed by everyone upon whom the change will impact, will enable effective evaluation to take place and any ongoing adjustments to be made.

4. Change is a personal process. For individuals, acceptance and ownership of change necessitates discovering its personal meaning. Accommodating change is a learning process, subject to an individual's learning styles and needs. As with all real learning, change demands risk-taking, working through periods of uncertainty and ambiguity in order to unfold new aspects, new dimensions of self.

5. Change is facilitated, not directed. Change agents require sensitivity and humility, recognising that they are merely part of a dynamic process which also contributes to their own personal growth. Facilitating change involves making connections, detecting potential for change and empowering individuals to act according to their beliefs and aspirations.

## B: Facilitating change in schools

6. *At a personal level*: change can be triggered by a range of events and experiences within and beyond school. 'Culture shock' – and the attendant confrontation with new values, perspectives and assumptions – can often precipitate change. In-school support is crucial for sustaining personal change, which involves risk-taking and uncertainty. In-service education which is whole-person oriented and sensitive to the holistic nature of change is a significant force for change.

7. *At a school level*: headteachers and senior staff can help facilitate change through sensitive and supportive leadership which acknowledges the multi-dimensional nature of change. Informal approaches – based on the 'ripple principle' – are very effective. Whole school change strategies should recognise the needs of the school community; they should be democratically conceived and realised, grounded in shared values and effectively sustained and monitored. Written school policies can legitimate and promote change, powerfully so if those within the institution have a stake in their formulation. In planning change, schools should be seen as part of a larger system, involving parents, the community and the local education authority.

8. *The local education authority's role*: individual LEA officers can be significant change agents, providing legitimation, encouragement and support. In-service courses need to be well-planned and executed, with good aftercare. The momentum they create should be sustained; the networking of teachers, schools and initiatives is a crucial means of so doing. LEA policies can provide an important umbrella of legitimation for change.

9. *The external agency's role*: external agencies are significant resource providers. This service could, however, be maximised with more effective dissemination of resources and training in their use. Strategies for achieving long-term whole school relationships need to be developed. External agencies often are crucial in-service providers, particularly if they have due regard for the complexity and subtlety of individual and institutional change processes.

# Bibliography

Baker, T., *et al.*, *Co-operating for a Change*, Newcastle-upon-Tyne LEA, 1987. A lively, well-presented set of classroom activities developed by Newcastle teachers working in conjunction with staff from the Centre for Global Education (See Case Study 9).

Bohm, D., *Wholeness and the Implicate Order*, Ark, 1983. This leading edge scientist explores his conception of the unity pervading everything. Essential, if difficult, reading.

Briggs, J. P., & Peat, F. D., *Looking Glass Universe. The Emerging Science of Wholeness*, Fontana, 1985. Fascinating exploration of how a number of prominent twentieth-century scientists have arrived at an holistic worldview as a result of their research.

Button, J., *A Dictionary of Green Ideas*, Routledge, 1988. A useful reference work bringing together most of the key concepts in the green view of the world.

Caldecott, L., & Leland, S., *Reclaim the Earth. Women Speak out for Life on Earth*, The Women's Press, 1983. An anthology of feminist writing on threats to life on Earth. Gives inspirational examples of women around the world working for change.

Capra, F., *The Tao of Physics*, Flamingo, 1976. Explores the parallels between the emergent holistic paradigm in sub-atomic physics and Eastern mysticism.

Capra, F., *The Turning Point. Science, Society and the Rising Culture*, Flamingo, 1983. A brilliant book; a turning point for many who read it. Explores how the fragmentationalist/mechanistic worldview of Descartes and Newton has led to the current global crisis and identifies an ongoing shift towards an holistic worldview.

Devall, B., & Sessions, G., *Deep Ecology. Living as if Nature Mattered*, Salt Lake City, Gibb M. Smith Inc., 1985. A thorough exploration of the concept of deep ecology as a radical alternative to the human-centred assumptions lying behind our thinking, attitudes and behaviours.

Dufty, D., & H., eds., *Thinking Whole. The Quest for a New Educational Paradigm*, Sydney, Social Education Association of Australia, 1988. Excellent collection of conference papers on holistic education prepared for the January 1988 Sydney 'Turning Point' Conference.

Dufty, D., & H., eds., *'The Turning Point' Conference. Looking Forward. Looking Back*, Sydney, Social Education Association of Australia, 1988. The sequel to *Thinking Whole*, it reflects the excitement and inspirational nature of the 'Turning Point' conference.

Ferguson, M., *The Aquarian Conspiracy. Personal and Social Transformation in the 1980s*, Granada, 1982. An account, painstaking in its detailed research, of the emergence of new paradigm thinking amongst groups from all walks of life. Their convergence, Ferguson argues, will lead to a radical change in Western culture.

Fox, M., *Original Blessing*, Santa Fe, New Mexico, Bean & Co., 1983. Offers a new religious/spiritual worldview aimed at re-uniting humankind with the planet.

Fox, M., & Swimme, B., *Manifesto for a Global Civilization*, Santa Fe, New Mexico, Bean & Co., 1982. Offers a vision of hope – from a Christian standpoint – for the birth of a new global civilization.

Fromm, E., *To Have or To Be?*, Abacus, 1979. A clear, philosophical exposition of the distinction between the 'having' mode of existence (the materialistic mode dominant in modern industrial society) and the 'being' mode (the ascendency of human over material values).

Fullan, M., *The Meaning of Educational Change*, New York, Teachers College Press, 1982. An important and influential book for anyone interested in change in education. Comprehensive in its survey of other literature on change, it puts forward crucial arguments about the importance of finding personal meaning in any change process.

Greig, S., Pike, G., & Selby, D., *Earthrights. Education as if the Planet Really Mattered*, Kogan Page/World Wide Fund For Nature UK, 1987. Offers an overview of current global problems and trends and explores the implications of the person/planet relationship for schools. Described by Jonathon Porritt as 'a superb handbook for teachers . . . which knocks spots off most other teaching aids in the area'.

Greig, S., Pike, G., & Selby, D., *Global Impact: First Year Report*, Centre for Global Education, 1987. A report on a questionnaire survey of schools and non-governmental organisations designed to find out about practice, policy and philosophy in development and environmental education.

Goodson, I. F., & Ball, S. J., eds., *Defining the Curriculum: Histories and Ethnographies*, Falmer Press, 1984. Interesting collection of articles taking an ethnographical approach to understanding the relationship between the teacher, the curriculum and change.

Heider, J., *The Tao of Leadership*, Wildwood House, 1986. Drawing upon various versions of the *Tao Te Ching*, it offers a manual on leadership for today's leaders. A must for chief education officers, advisers, headteachers, deputy headteachers, heads of department and inset facilitators.

Higgins, R., *The Seventh Enemy. The Human Factor in the Global Crisis*, Pan, 1980. Identifies six threats to human survival, all of which are soluble if we could only overcome the seventh – moral blindness coupled with political inertia.

Lipnack, J., & Stamps, J., *The Networking Book. People Connecting with People*, Routledge & Kegan Paul, 1986. Thoroughgoing exploration of the philosophy and process of global networking.

Lovelock, J. E., *Gaia. A New Look at Life on Earth*, Oxford University Press, 1982. Investigates the hypothesis that the Earth forms a single complex and conscious system which defines and maintains conditions necessary for its own survival.

Miller, J., *The Holistic Curriculum*, Ontario, OISE Press, 1988. A comprehensive and lucid exposition of the aims and substance of holistic education, based on a thoroughgoing analysis of historical attempts to provide an holistic curriculum.

Muller, R., *New Genesis. Shaping a Global Spirituality*, New York, Image, 1984. Challenging, optimistic statement of the author's vision of the transition to global harmony. Chapter on 'The need for global education'.

Parsons, C., *The Curriculum Change Game*, Falmer Press, 1987. As a longitudinal study of the Schools Council GYSL project, this book provides a rare in-depth insight into the design, dissemination and impact of a major curriculum project. Useful introductory and summary chapters on educational change.

Pietroni, P., *Holistic Living. A Guide to Self-Care by a Leading Practitioner*, Dent, 1986. Practical advice on how to look after the whole person. Some excellent insights into humanity's relationship with the environment.

Pike, G., & Selby, D., *Global Teacher, Global Learner*, Hodder & Stoughton, 1987. Reconceptualises the term global education, examines appropriate teaching and learning styles and offers a range of primary and secondary classroom activities.

Porritt, J., *Seeing Green. The Politics of Ecology Explained*, Basil Blackwell, 1984. A delightfully lucid survey of contemporary ecological thinking.

Porritt, J., & Winner, D., *The Coming of the Greens*, Fontana, 1988. Examines how green thinking has begun to pervade all aspects of British society in recent years.

Reason, P., & Rowan, J., *Human Inquiry: A Sourcebook of New Paradigm Research*, John Wiley & Sons, 1981. An authoritative source of writing on approaches to research in the human sciences which are collaborative and experiential – important aspects of any evaluation of holistic education.

Richardson, R., 'Changing the Curriculum', in Hicks, D., ed., *Education for Peace: Issues, Principles and Practice in the Classroom*, Routledge, 1983. Brief but useful chapter summarising some major points arising from academic writing on educational change, then offering a thought-provoking critique from an anti-racist perspective.

Rifkin, J., *Entropy. A New World View*, Paladin, 1985. A critique of the fragmentationalist and materialist worldview. Offers an alternative worldview grounded in the Entropy Law (which states that available energy is decreasing for the universe as a whole) and asks us to consider its social, educational, political, economic and personal implications.

Robertson, J., *The Sane Alternative. A Choice of Futures*, James Robertson, Spring Cottage, 9 New Road, Ironbridge, Shropshire TF8 7AU. Explores alternative futures and, in particular, Robertson's conception of a Sane, Humane and Ecological (SHE) future.

Roszak, T., *Person/Planet*, Granada, 1981. A brilliant and inspirational work linking together two powerful contemporary movements – the exploration of human potential and emergent planetary awareness. Superb chapter on education.

Russell, P., *The Awakening Earth. Our Next Evolutionary Leap*, Routledge & Kegan Paul, 1982. Puts forward the idea of the Earth as a self-regulatory organism and considers human potential through, as it were, the eyes of the planet.

Sarason, S., *The Culture of the School and the Problem of Change*, Allyn & Bacon, 1982. This book provides a sound and cogently argued rationale for the need to fully understand the realities of day-to-day school life if we are ever to promote change more effectively.

Schwarz, W., & D., *Breaking Through. Theory and Practice of Wholistic Living*, Green Books, 1987. A well-written account of how green/holistic ideas are surfacing and having an impact in many different parts of society.

Seed, J., Macy, J., Fleming, P., Naess, A., *Thinking Like a Mountain. Towards a Council of All Beings*, Heretic Books, 1988. A collection of readings, meditations, poems, guided fantasies, workshop notes and drawings designed to help us experience our oneness with nature.

Sloan, D., ed., *Toward the Recovery of Wholeness. Knowledge, Education and Human Values*, New York, Teachers College Press, 1984. Collection of important papers on holistic thinking presented at a 1980 symposium at Woodstock, Vermont. Especially valuable are the papers by David Bohm and Huston Smith.

Smith, H., *Beyond the Post-Modern Mind*, Wheaton, Illinois, Theosophical Publishing House, 1982. A plea for the Western world to look beyond its materialistic culture, to relinquish its 'power over nature' approach to life and to explore our inner nature and potential.

Spretnak, C., & Capra, F., *Green Politics. The Global Promise*, Paladin, 1986. Offers an insight into Green politics in Western Germany and their relevance to the wider world.

Weber, R., *Dialogues with Scientists and Sages: The Search for Unity*, Routledge & Kegan Paul, 1987. Contemporary scientists and mystics share their views on space, time, matter, energy, life, consciousness, nature and human beings' place in the scheme of things. An inspirational source for those wanting to explore holistic thinking in depth.

Weston, J., ed., *Red and Green. The New Politics of the Environment*, Pluto, 1986. Makes the case that for Green politics to work, a social policy is needed which views capitalist industry as the primary cause of environmental destruction.

Zukav, G., *The Dancing Wu Li Masters. An Overview of the New Physics*, Bantam, 1979. A clear, easy-to-read, account of developments in sub-atomic physics which have led physicists to see the world in new, holistic ways.

# Index